I really liked this book. I couldn't set it down. I got done reading it and I just wanted to read it again so I did.

– Cole, 11

I've read all the Brady Street Boys books and I think each one gets better. Maybe because I feel like I know the boys personally. I never really thought about what longsuffering means until they lived it out in their lives. I like all the adventures the boys get into and I wish I had been their brother!

– Wade, 10

This book is great! You are in such great suspense and you can hardly read fast enough.

– Alyssa, 11

I really enjoyed this book, especially the parts about hobos.

– Robin, 11

I really like these books because of the suspense that causes you to keep on reading while wondering what is going to happen next.

– Erika, 12

This is a work of fiction. Names, characters, places, and incidents either are the product of the author's imagination or are used fictitiously.

With any questions write to
Katrina Lee
The Brady Street Boys
PO Box 2155
Elkhart, IN 46515

First edition 2022

Book design by Viewfinder Creative
Illustrations by Josh Tufts
Maps by Rebecca Hoover and Taya Timm

ISBN 978-1-958683-01-9 (paperback)
ISBN 978-1-958683-02-6 (ebook)

www.katrinahooverlee.com

THE BRADY STREET BOYS

Book 4: Tricked on the Tracks

written by Katrina Hoover Lee

BRADY STREET BOYS SERIES THEMES

Book 1 || Trapped in the Tunnel.................... ***Love***
Book 2 || Facing the Fugitive........................... ***Joy***
Book 3 || Noise in the Night........................ ***Peace***
Book 4 || Tricked on the Tracks...... ***Longsuffering***
Book 5 || .... ***Gentleness***
Book 6 || .... ***Goodness***
Book 7 || .... ***Faith***
Book 8 || .... ***Meekness***
Book 9 || .... ***Temperance***

But the fruit of the Spirit is
love, joy, peace, longsuffering,
gentleness, goodness, faith,
meekness, temperance:
against such there is no law.
Galatians 5:22-23

The Brady Street Boys Adventure Series

Terry, Gary and Larry Fitzpatrick live in northern Indiana along the St. Joseph River. President Reagan lives in the White House. Gasoline costs 90 cents a gallon. For families like the Fitzpatricks, computers and cell phones are still things of the future. The boys' Christian parents teach them to pray and give them a project to learn the fruit of the Spirit. They help Gary navigate the pain of losing his leg and his firefighting dreams.

But having a wooden leg doesn't keep Gary from adventures. With Terry the acrobat, and Larry the brain, Gary begins a quest to find an answer to the most important mystery of all.

What happened to the surgeon who amputated Gary's leg, and has now disappeared?

Contents

LEXINGTON BRIDGE
OUR HOUSE
NUMBER TEN
TINA'S HOUSE
BRADY STREET
BRADY STREET NEIGHBORHOOD
LIBRARY
MAIN STREET
STRATFORD LIBRARY
GROCERY
EAT

Gary's Map of the Neighborhood
ST. JOSEPH RIVER
DAD'S SHOP
ROCKY'S RIVERSIDE RESTAURANT
ROCKY'S
Milton's
MILTON'S ICE CREAM SHOP

Common Hobo Symbols

Source: https://www.nsa.gov/portals/75/documents/about/cryptologic-heritage/museum/hobo-signs-definitions.pdf

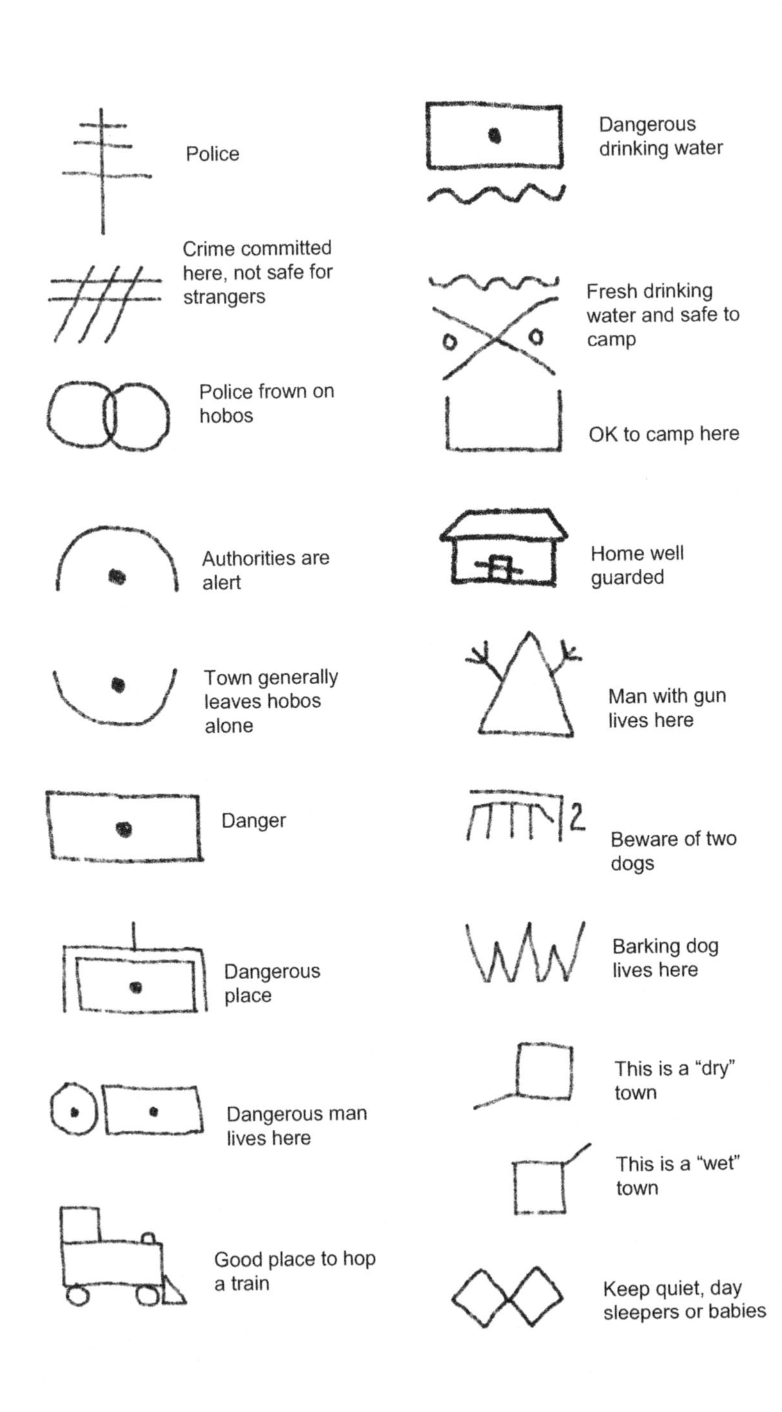
Police
Dangerous drinking water
Crime committed here, not safe for strangers
Fresh drinking water and safe to camp
Police frown on hobos
OK to camp here
Authorities are alert
Home well guarded
Town generally leaves hobos alone
Man with gun lives here
Danger
2
Beware of two dogs
Dangerous place
Barking dog lives here
This is a "dry" town
Dangerous man lives here
This is a "wet" town
Good place to hop a train
Keep quiet, day sleepers or babies

CHAPTER ONE

Dean's Home

"Do you know which apartment he lives in?" Uncle Aaron's voice came from the gloom above my head.

I looked up at Uncle Aaron. My eyes traveled past the top of his head to the dull electric light hanging from the ceiling behind the crossbars of a dusty spiderweb. Compared to the light outside, it was almost dark. My eyes adjusted further, and I saw my brothers, Terry and Larry, both looking at me.

"Why are you looking at me? I don't know where he lives."

I guess we were all expecting Dean to come running out when we drove up. The previous afternoon, we had met him at the tennis court to fly kites and make plans for today. Now it was today, and we realized we had forgotten to make our plans thoroughly enough. We had arranged to pick Dean up at 9 a.m., but we had not asked for his apartment number. And he was nowhere to be seen.

Worry pried at my insides like a robber coming to steal my peace, rattling the latches of my mood.

This was to be the moment we picked up Dr. Jefferson's trail. Dean had identified the meaning of CHEL. It was a train. Not a passenger train, which offered tickets to riders, but a freight train for hauling coal and steel machinery and tankers of oil. We could hear the horns of passing trains from our house, although we weren't close to the tracks. Some nights the train horns sounded as if they came from just across the Lexington Street Bridge. Other days, we could barely hear them. I had never thought about the men who hopped on the trains to get a free ride. Mom had told us once that people jumped on trains a lot more back in the Depression days when our grandparents were young. It didn't happen so much anymore.

A train-hopping hobo. Was that really Dr. Jefferson?

I knew a few basic details about Dr. Jefferson.

1. He was the surgeon who had amputated my leg when I was seven years old, ending my dreams of becoming a firefighter.
2. When my mom reached out to find him so I could ask him questions about the surgery, she was told he had disappeared.
3. When we visited his office, they told us my documents had disappeared too.

4. When we met an international art thief, he said he had a friend named Bruce who worked with artificial limbs and had taken the CHEL.

We would never know what had happened to Dr. Jefferson or why he had quit medical work. Not until we found him. And Dean was going to help us find him, now that we knew the CHEL was a freight train. He was going with us to the Hobo Jungle to track down his uncle, a hobo. Since he was a hobo, he might have met Dr. Jefferson.

But first we had to find Dean.

The apartment building we were standing in smelled like cats and cigarette smoke. I had only one thought as the front door whined shut, and we stood in the gloom inside the apartment complex. *Dean lives here?* I felt sick, almost lightheaded, as I inhaled the depressing air.

"Well, I suggest we knock on someone's door and ask," Uncle Aaron said. "Some of the residents probably know each other."

Uncle Aaron normally worked with concrete. Muscles rippled in his arms from the heavy work. He was visiting us on his vacation, which he had originally planned to use on a mission trip. But he had injured his back at work and was needing to take it easy.

I would never have thought of trying random doors in the apartment, but it was a great idea.

Bang. Bang. Bang.

Uncle Aaron's fist thudded against the first wooden door

inside the main entrance. He had no hesitation, no fear. He just did what the situation required.

The door he knocked on had a crooked wooden 3 hanging by a loose nail. The number was once painted gold. But, like the rest of the apartment, it was deteriorating. The gold paint had come off in patches, and the numeral looked like an exotic spotted animal. Suddenly, the 3 jumped sideways. The entire door burst open with a harsh sound like a person coughing.

I don't know who was more surprised, the lady at the door or the four of us standing there looking at her. She was a large woman with a cigarette in her mouth and a box of cornflakes in her hands.

"Do ya need something?" Her voice was deep, almost like a man's.

"Good morning, ma'am." Uncle Aaron smiled at the woman. "I don't know if you can help us, but we are looking for a friend, a boy named Dean who lives in this building. We failed to get his apartment number. Would you happen to know him or his family and where he lives?"

The woman removed the cigarette from her mouth. "I'm the manager here, so I guess I know my people."

"Great!" Uncle Aaron's voice sounded truly thankful. "I'm glad we found you. Can you point us in the right direction?"

The woman actually returned the smile, then waved her cigarette at the staircase behind us. "Up the stairs. First door on the right at the top of the stairs. Number eight."

"Thank you so much," Uncle Aaron said. "I'm sure managing

a place like this is difficult work."

The woman laughed a wheezy, gravelly laugh. "You're sure, are you? Well, you're right about that!"

"Is there anything particularly stressful right now?" Uncle Aaron asked.

The woman seemed surprised by the question.

"Waall, the family visiting Dean's mom right now is stressing me out," she said. "Woman asked me for an apartment but there ain't no room here. There's no way I can help her, even though she said she would have to sleep on the streets."

"That does sound difficult. I'll pray about that," Uncle Aaron said. "Thanks for your help."

The woman nodded, then carefully placed the cigarette back in her mouth and shut the door in our faces without another word.

We turned, and Terry led the way up the stairs. Going up stairs with a wooden leg is not the easiest thing in the world, although it isn't the hardest either. It would have helped a lot if Dr. Jefferson had only removed the lower part of my leg. But according to Mom, the cancer had been in my knee too.

But had Dr. Jefferson even been telling the truth to my parents? Why were my documents and the surgeon missing?

My eyes had adjusted, so the second floor seemed much brighter. A green numeral 8 on the door at the top of the stairs was fastened tightly in place by two small nails and had no missing paint.

I was so busy admiring the 8 that for a second I didn't register the voice.

"I have my own child to raise!" a voice shouted.

"Dean is thirteen! He's not a child!"

Actually, there were a few other words in the dialogue too, all of which our parents had expressly forbidden us to use or repeat.

We were standing in front of the 8 door, shifting from foot to foot, uncomfortable. Dean's mom was talking to the visitor the apartment manager had mentioned.

"We'd better knock." Uncle Aaron looked at the door. "I hate to interrupt, but it's worse to stand here listening."

Uncle Aaron adjusted his knock to a polite tap, knowing there were people close by who could answer the door.

The shouting stopped.

"Who's that?" someone mumbled.

The door coughed open like the one below, and there was Dean's mom. The smell of fried eggs mingled with the smell of cigarette smoke. Behind her, I saw a sagging couch in front of a large TV, and a bank of clothes piled beside the couch. An outdoor garden wind vane leaned against the TV, as if to test the direction of the conversations. There was no sign of Dean—or anyone else.

I could hardly look at Dean's mom without remembering her screaming at Dean for not stealing enough toilet paper. But I tried to dispel the memory. Close up, she looked like a mom who would bake cookies and play board games. She had brown hair and eyes, like Dean's. Not fat, not thin, and clean clothes. The green paint on her fingernails matched the green of her wristwatch.

I was trying to remember if we knew her name when she said, in a very unhelpful tone, "Can I help you?"

"Yes, we're friends of Dean's." I heard my own voice babbling. "Is he ready to go?"

"Go? He's not going anywhere. He's not here."

Her eyes flitted to Uncle Aaron and to my brothers and then back at me, as if daring me to ask for anything further. Uncle Aaron rescued me.

"Do you know if he's close by? We can pick him up somewhere else. He agreed to introduce us to his uncle, since we want to talk to a hobo."

"Buckle is not a hobo! He's a zookeeper!"

We stared at Dean's mom. I'm sure we looked like a bunch of owls in the bird section of the zoo.

"A zookeeper?" I heard my own voice croaking out the question.

"Yes, and I'm upset that you call my brother Buckle a hobo. But anyway, Dean is busy. I'm a little busy myself. Thank you for stopping by."

Wham!

For the second time that day, a door was shut in our faces.

CHAPTER TWO

The Rail Yard

This truly did switch off my current of excitement. We stared at each other, then slowly descended the stairs and stepped out the front door. It swung shut, metal screeching against metal as if it wasn't installed properly.

"What do we do now?" I almost wailed. What was going on? Had Dean actually lied to us, both about his Uncle Buckle and about his willingness to go with us to the train yard?

A light drizzle had started in the short time we were inside the apartment, just enough to make the world ugly and gloomy and turn the dust in the parking lot into mud that coated the soles of our shoes and rubbed off on the floor mats and vinyl of Uncle Aaron's clean Camaro.

"What kind of a name is Buckle?" Larry asked from the back seat.

"Probably a nickname," Uncle Aaron said. "Hmmm. A zookeeper."

"So, Dean lied to us." Terry didn't think it was a question.

I was in the front seat beside Uncle Aaron because it was my turn. We had devised an age-based rotating system. Terry had ridden up front on the way to Dean's apartment, so it was now my turn. The next time we went somewhere, it would be Larry's turn.

Terry had tried to make the point that since he was fourteen years old and taller than both of us, he should automatically get the passenger's seat full-time. Larry, the intelligent one, said that was ridiculous and at the most Terry should get a few extra moments in the front. I had pulled out my notebook and done some quick figuring based on our ages.

1. Terry was 14. I was 13. Larry was 12.
2. Larry was $12/14$ Terry's age.
3. I was $13/14$ Terry's age.
4. So Larry should get $6/7$ as much time in the front seat as Terry and I would get $13/14$ as much time as Terry did.

I was doing the math to figure out what $13/14$ of an hour was, when Uncle Aaron shook his head and suggested that we take turns. Terry didn't love the idea, but he hated doing math even more, so we had compromised and accepted Uncle Aaron's suggestion.

"Where to now, Gary?" Uncle Aaron turned the key in the ignition and the engine hummed to life. "Should we go search the train yard anyway?"

I wasn't exactly in charge of the expedition, but he knew how badly I wanted to find out about Dr. Jefferson. My brothers were interested, too, ever since the surgeon's office told us that he had disappeared and the documents about my surgery were gone. But I was the one who cared the most. For instance, what if Dr. Jefferson was actually a criminal who had been cutting off people's legs when there was nothing wrong with them? If that were the case, I didn't know if I wanted to find out. But at the same time, I had to. I had to know.

Worse, the clue that finally connected us with Dr. Jefferson's next step had come from a criminal–the international fugitive who specialized in stealing ancient artifacts. So even if Dr. Jefferson was not a criminal, he had been known to hang out with professional thieves.

We headed toward Elkhart. Uncle Aaron turned on his wipers, and I watched them push the drops of drizzle off to the side and top of the windshield, where they wandered off like miniature versions of our favorite river. I knew the St. Joseph River was running along beside us, but we couldn't see it behind the houses and trees at the side of the road.

"Don't anyone mention it." Terry spoke warily, as if he were discussing a criminal trial that had possibly been called off. "But I think maybe Mom forgot to give us the next fruit of the Spirit project. I thought she was going to give us our assignment yesterday and she never did."

"She'll remember." I turned away from the side window and looked back at my brothers.

"Or she thinks we're so responsible we'll keep an eye out for long-suffering people on our own," Larry said.

"Is long-suffering the next one?" Terry said. "That's easy for me in this back seat. I'm long and I'm suffering."

Uncle Aaron laughed and reached back to slap Terry on the knee. "If that's the worst thing that ever requires long-suffering on your part, you'll live an easy life."

"Hey, look!" Larry was sitting behind me, leaning against his window. "The train cars! Is this the beginning of the rail yard?"

"Looks like it." Uncle Aaron moved his eyes from the road, to the train cars, then back to the road. "I suppose I missed my turn to get in there. Oh well, we'll drive ahead and see what we can find."

When Larry said *Hey look!* I had turned my head to the right as well. As I watched the tops of the railcars flash past the window, a nervous jitter started inside my stomach as if I had swallowed a dragonfly that was just regaining consciousness and beginning to thrash.

What if Dr. Jefferson was in that rail yard somewhere, hunkered down in a car? If he was, why was he there?

I clutched the handle on the door to steady myself and reviewed a few important facts.

1. None of us would recognize Dr. Jefferson if we

saw him. It was six years since we had seen him.

2. Even though we now had good reason to think that Dr. Jefferson had jumped on the CHEL freight train from Chicago to Elkhart, we had no idea when he had done this.

3. Even though we thought Dr. Jefferson had come on the CHEL, we could be wrong.

4. The international fugitive could have been lying. Or, possibly he could have been talking about a different friend named Bruce who worked with artificial legs.

With these calming thoughts I quieted my internal dragonfly as Uncle Aaron took a right turn onto busy Nappanee Street in Elkhart.

"Okay, we're going under the tracks now," Uncle Aaron said. "And we have passed the rail yard, so we want to turn back down a side road to see if we can get to it."

We passed through the gloom of the short tunnel under the train bridge and came out by a bank of green grass sloping up to a small cluster of trees. Right past the trees, a road turned back the way we had come.

"Lusher Avenue. Okay, this way I think." Uncle Aaron turned right.

Ahead we saw train cars, buildings, and a large frame structure above several tracks that looked as if a person could stand on it and look down on the trains. A square building towered out ahead. On the right, several tracks went straight into several huge sheds with overhead doors.

"Whoa," Uncle Aaron said. "It looks quite big. You didn't tell me about the size of this place."

"That's because we didn't know either," I said. "We've never been here before."

It was a huge place and slightly intimidating.

"I'm wondering if this is even a public road," Uncle Aaron said. "Oh well. The most they can do is tell us to leave. Obviously, the hobos come here uninvited."

"Look at those sheds that the trains can drive into," Larry said. "I read in a book that sometimes hobos accidentally get

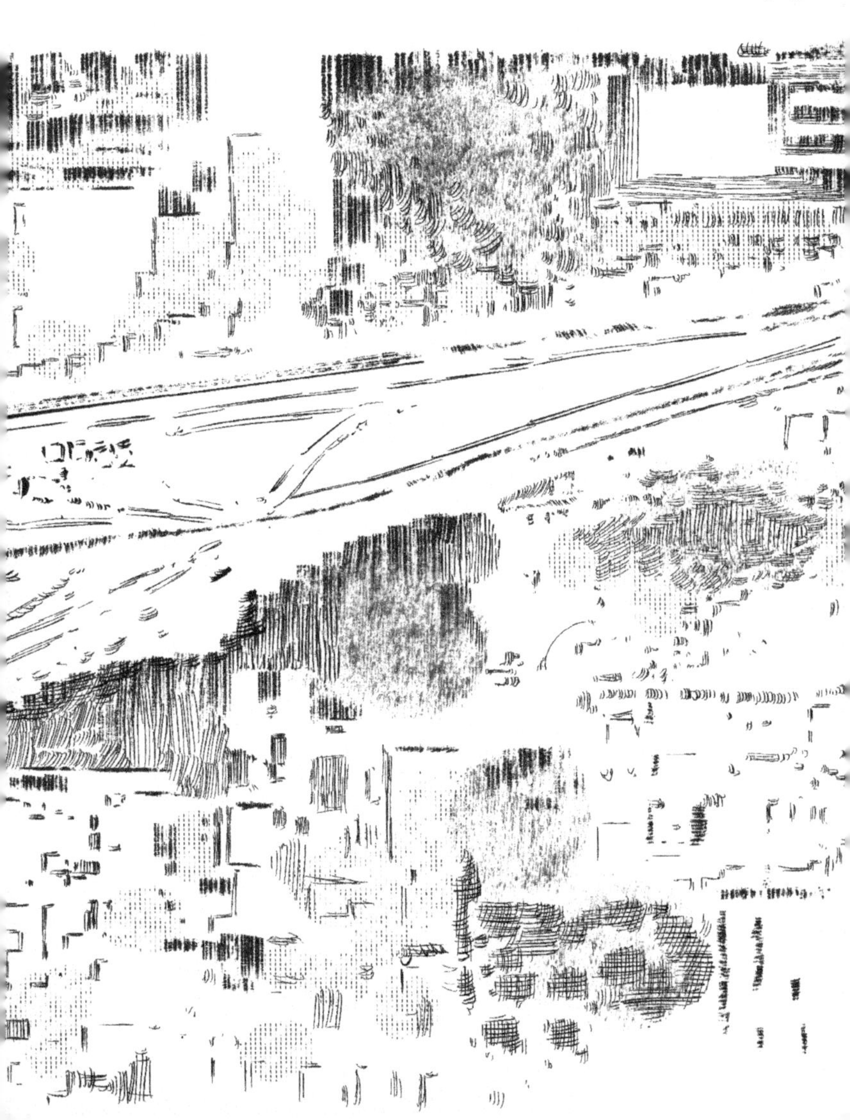

locked in boxcars, and then someone shunts the car off into the warehouse because it isn't needed anymore. They starve to death in there."

"I'm sure it's never happened here." I couldn't help but look at the sheds, but I really didn't want to think about it. Larry reads too much for his own good.

Uncle Aaron drove around for a bit looking for a main entrance, but we couldn't see anything marked as such. Finally, he parked in a lot with other vehicles, beside a block building that looked most likely to contain an office. We piled out.

As we approached the buildings, we saw an exterior steel stairway leading to the second floor.

"Maybe that's the office." Uncle Aaron nodded toward the top floor. "Let's find out."

He took the stairs, still damp from the rain, two at a time. Suddenly he stopped short and grabbed his back.

"Forgot again." He rubbed his back and winced, then moved more slowly up the stairs.

When we arrived on the wooden platform in front of the door, he knocked. It was a little crowded up there, and I hoped the platform would hold.

No one came. Uncle Aaron knocked again.

"I hate to disappoint you," he said, glancing at me. "But I'm not sure this place is open to the public. Don't be too discouraged if no one comes to the door or they run us off."

I was thinking about how nice it was that the drizzle had stopped when the door burst open, revealing a large security officer. The word large is not sufficient, really. His face loomed above us like the top of a small water tower. He had fingers like plumbing pipes and a nose like a faucet. He held the largest pencil I had ever seen. It was exceptionally wide, as if he found it impossible to hang onto the normal size.

"Excuse me?"

Even his voice was big. It came from so close to the top of the door frame that I took another look. He would never make it out the door without ducking.

Uncle Aaron cleared his throat. "Is there an office here at the train yard open to the public? We have a couple of questions."

When he said this, I realized we hadn't discussed what we would ask. That was the beauty of having an adult along, and I was sure hoping he had a plan.

"What kind of questions?" The large man bit into the eraser of the pencil.

"Well." Uncle Aaron cleared his throat again. "Gary, do you want me to carry on, or do you want to do the talking?"

"Go ahead," I said.

"Okay, we are looking for a hobo, actually." Uncle Aaron laughed a little to signal to the big man that he knew hobos were not exactly on the rail yard roster.

"Are you a hobo?" He took a step back into the room, removing the pencil from his mouth. Behind him I saw a desk with a large metal fan behind that. On one side of the desk, I saw a large wooden cabinet with wide, thin drawers. A map flopped from one drawer, and I concluded it must be a map cabinet. Below us, I heard men's voices calling and the clacking of metal tools.

"No, we aren't hobos," Uncle Aaron assured him. "We are looking for a doctor who we suspect hopped a train from Chicago. But even if he's not here anymore we thought there might be some other hobos around who would have met him."

"We don't have any office here for finding hobos," the guard grunted. "Just a second."

The radio on his belt crackled and he turned a dial with a practiced hand, increasing the volume. *Be advised to watch for a young woman who is wanted for drug trafficking.* Static buzzed. *Elkhart police are looking for her.* More static, like our lawn mower hitting a patch of weeds. *Believe she hopped trains in the past.*

"Description?" The big guard stepped back into the room and grabbed a yellow writing pad, large size, and began jotting down information with the pencil.

Posting photo on the board. Very small woman, about 100 pounds, tattoo of a heart on her cheek.

"Copy." The guard turned the volume lower again, jotted down a few more lines, and looked at us as if he could not believe we existed. "As you can see, we have plenty of issues with hobos without keeping track of their names or where they come from."

If it would have been just me, I would have apologized and run away. But Uncle Aaron kept pressing.

"I understand," he said. "Could you point us in the right direction for where we might find some hobos to talk to?"

"Not my job description. Some of 'em used to sleep up at the corner." The guard pointed a fat finger over Uncle Aaron's shoulder. "Hobo Jungle. In the trees right by the underpass."

"Okay, great, we'll check it out."

I was more than ready to exit the place and led the way down the steps, leaping from stair to stair on my good leg.

"I thought we were going to jail ourselves there for a little," I said when we were all at the bottom heading for the car.

"Oh no," Uncle Aaron laughed. "He was a little irritated, but I've been a lot closer to going to jail than that."

"Like when?" we all asked at once.

Uncle Aaron laughed uproariously this time. "I'm mostly joking."

I loved listening to Uncle Aaron's stories. He loved action and adventure, especially if it involved helping other people. Nothing scared him.

We drove back out Lusher Avenue almost all the way to Nappanee Street. Uncle Aaron pulled off and parked the car in the weeds beside the road. The railroad man had not been sure that any hobos still stayed here. But they must have—if Dean wasn't lying to us.

"Ready?" Uncle Aaron opened the driver's door. "Hobo Jungle, here we come."

CHAPTER THREE

The Hobo Jungle

As we got out of the car, the rain started up again. It wasn't a cold day, thankfully. But it was turning out to be a wet one.

"Here's a path!" Terry shouted from the other side of the road. Sure enough, the grass was matted down, and patches of dirt showed, sticky black from the rain. Pieces of colored paper and gum wrappers peeked at us from the grass and dirt. We all followed Terry up the slightly sloping path toward the trees between us and the railroad tracks that crossed the busy street. As we got closer to the trees, we saw signs of life. A blue tarp fastened to several trees for a shelter. White five-gallon buckets lying on their sides and cluttered with clothes, toothpaste and toilet paper as if they were makeshift cabinets. In front of the tarp, we saw one lone man, smoking a pipe and watching us approach. His tangled beard and wild hair sprouting under a cowboy hat suddenly made me nervous. Was he about to whip out a Colt revolver, leap to his feet, shout out a war cry, jump onto a horse, and take off, firing at us?

He did not.

Instead, he just kept watching us and the closer we got, the more I wondered when we should be saying something. Thankfully, Uncle Aaron saved the day again.

"Good morning, sir!"

The hobo took his pipe out of his mouth, slowly blew out a cloud of smoke, and rested both hands on his knees. "Morning."

By the time he got to the greeting, we were ducking under the branches at the edge of the clearing. Drops of rainwater landed on us as we disturbed the foliage. I felt the beginning of a small creek meander down my neck and back. I sure hoped this man knew Dr. Jefferson, or all this trouble wasn't going to be worthwhile. Smoke curled up from a campfire across the clearing. A patched blue tarp covered a pile of something on the right side of the campfire, the bristles of a yellow broom protruding from under the tarp.

By this time, the hairy man was motioning us under the tarp with him. He scooted his five-gallon bucket to the edge of the dry patch under the tarp.

"Don't got enough empty buckets," he said. "But ya'll can stand or sit on the ground. It's a bit of a one-man site, I dare say."

"No problem," Uncle Aaron said. "I have a bad back right now so I think I'll stay standing, but the boys might have a seat." He motioned to the ground as if he thought it might be a good

idea if we accepted the man's hospitality. So we did.

"Looks like that one's got a bad leg," the man said to Uncle Aaron.

"Yes, I do," I answered. If there was anything I hated more than losing my leg, it was when people spoke about it as if I wasn't there. "It's actually a wooden leg."

The man nodded gravely, then put the stem of his pipe back between his teeth as if it were easier to do that than think of something to say.

"Gary, on that note, maybe you can tell him who you are looking for. My name is Aaron by the way," our uncle said, extending a hand to the hobo.

"And my name is Old Fish." The old man took his hand and shook it soberly. "They call me that because I eat bugs like a fish."

"You do?" Larry stared at him with amazement. I suppose we all had that owl look again.

"Got to have protein, now, don't I?" He chuckled. "Just grasshoppers mostly, like people ate in the Bible. My mama used to read me those stories during the Depression."

I thought of asking if fish eat grasshoppers, but it didn't seem to the point. After a brief silence, Uncle Aaron left the buggy topic and got back to business.

"These boys are my nephews. We're looking for...Wait, I'm not the one who should tell the story." Uncle Aaron prodded me with his shoe. "Go for it."

"We are looking for the doctor who amputated my leg," I said. "I was hoping to talk to him so I could understand the surgery better, but we were told he disappeared. Later, we figured out he came to Elkhart on a freight train, the CHEL."

"From Chicago." Old Fish nodded and spoke the words around the stem of the pipe.

"And then our friend Dean said his uncle is a hobo who might have known Dr. Jefferson."

Old Fish frowned.

"What's this uncle's name?"

"Buckle, I think."

"We were going to bring Dean with us," Larry said. "But he didn't show up this morning."

The old man chuckled, and it sounded like he had a mug of rocks in his throat. "The makings of a great hobo. Failure to appear when expected."

A comment this witty surprised me, but the man was probably right about Dean's odds of becoming a hobo, unfortunately.

"I'd say there's five to ten of us around right now. Used to be so many more, back in the 60s and 70s," the man went on. "Buckle comes around sometimes, but he's not here now."

"Oh, he does?" I looked up at Uncle Aaron. "Then Dean wasn't lying!"

"I don't think he's a doctor," Old Fish said. "Don't look like one anyways. He's a big red-faced man that blinks a lot. Strange old man, that one."

Uncle Aaron explained that we didn't think Buckle was a doctor, but that we were hoping he knew the doctor who had become a hobo.

Old Fish chewed on the stem of his pipe. "You think a doctor rode the rails out?"

"We think he did." My voice wavered. His question made me wonder. Would a doctor, whether a good one or a bad one, live like Old Fish?

"Could be, could be," the old man conceded, as if he had read my mind and wanted to calm my fears. "There's a little hobo in everyone from time to time. Seems like that's all people do anymore is just hop a train for one or two trips. Hardly any real hobos what travel their whole life anymore these days. People have it too nice, I guess. All these new-fangled conventions like air conditioning."

"Did you ever know anyone who got locked in a boxcar and died?" Larry sat on the packed earth, wrists on his knees, eyes shining. He was in his element to be talking to a real hobo, and I knew he couldn't help asking the question. I was just glad he hadn't corrected Old Fish and told him he meant *inventions* instead of *conventions.*

Old Fish chuckled again with the rattling noise. "Didn't happen to me." He said it like a boast, puffing his chest out a little. "Heard of it, but never knew no one who died that way. We don't die much anymore, not like they did in the old days falling off trains and getting run over and stuff."

"Is it true that hobos use a secret code to communicate with each other?" Larry asked next. I was irritated with him. Him and his reading. He was always full of questions. Did he have to dominate the conversation? What on earth did he mean about a secret code?

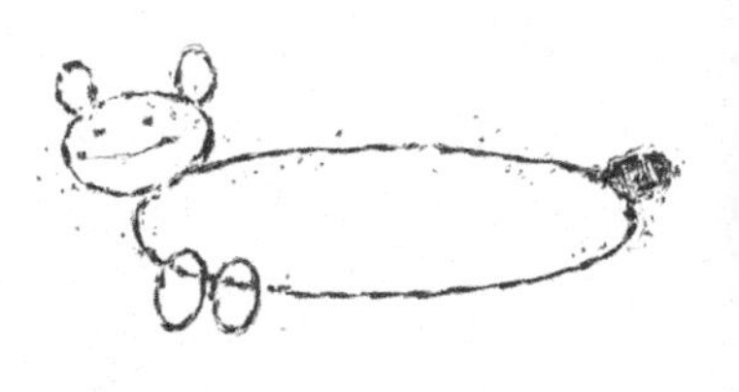

"Oh, yeah, sometimes," the old man said. "Like drawing a cat on the door where there's a nice woman that gives people food. Yup, sure."

"Can you draw us some?" Larry asked next.

I almost groaned. "Wait, Larry. Shouldn't we be seeing if we can find anything out about Dr. Jefferson?"

The old man leaned down off his bucket and reached for a stick at the edge of the clearing. It was just out of his reach, but Terry jumped up and got it for him. For a second I thought maybe he was going to beat me up with it for interrupting.

"But we tried." Larry looked like he was totally surprised that I wasn't fascinated by the symbols. "He doesn't know him."

"Nope, don't think there's a doctor around," the hobo repeated.

Uncle Aaron chimed in from above, close to the tarp. His voice seemed a little louder than normal, as if it was bouncing off the roof. "This might have been a while ago that he arrived. Do you remember a doctor here, say in the last six months, maybe the last year?"

"I come and I go." Old Fish smoothed the dirt at his feet with a scuffed cowboy boot. "So I'm not always here." Then he picked up the stick. "This here means *safe camp,*" he said, scratching in the dirt. He scratched three lines and put two eyes on his figure like a face. It was as if he had tuned out the question about Dr. Jefferson. He scratched a cross in the ground. "And then this

one here means *talk religion, get food.*" He drew a pole with a curvy line around it. "This means *help if sick.*" He smoothed the dirt out again and started fresh.

"Here's one for you." Old Fish looked at me before drawing again. He drew an X and added a face like a head at the top. "This means *the doctor lives here.*"

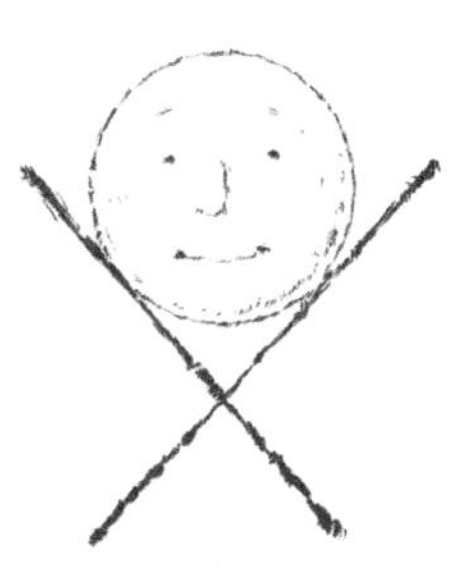

I found myself growing intrigued even though I was disappointed Old Fish didn't know the doctor we wanted to find.

"Do people actually pretend to like religion to get food?" I asked.

"Maybe they don't pretend, maybe they do like it," the man said. "Just because we're hobos doesn't mean we ain't got religion. I told you my monica is Old Fish. You know how fish go with religion?"

"What do you mean by Monica?" Larry asked. "Isn't that a woman's name?"

"No, just a name."

Larry frowned, puzzled.

"I thought you said they called you Old Fish because you eat bugs," Terry said.

"Well, that's in the Bible too, didn't I tell you? Eating bugs is religion too." Old Fish used the stick to scratch a fish into the dirt and added an arrow. "Say I decide to leave today and want to let the others know that aren't here right now but might come back. I'd scratch this fish here with an arrow pointing whatever direction I went."

Larry evaluated the arrow. "So that means you'd be getting on a westbound train."

The rocks rattled again as Old Fish chuckled. "Gotta be careful with those words, boy," he said. "When people die, they say he 'caught the Westbound.' Better to say, going west."

"Oh!" Larry said. "And why is this called a hobo jungle? It doesn't really look like a jungle, as there aren't many trees. And I don't see any parrots."

"You might be surprised how many colorful birds come through here." The old man chuckled again. "Colorful birds and old fish. Other hobo that's been around a long time goes by Crumb Boss. He had a pet crow years ago that always went with him ever'where he went. He picked up the crumbs all over and even brought his owner some food once. So they called the bird Crumb Boss, but when the bird died they started calling the man Crumb Boss. His monica is a crow. I'd know it anywhere."

"What if you don't want people to know where you are?" Uncle Aaron stretched his shoulders to left and right. "I'm surprised hobos mark where they are going for everyone to see if riding trains is illegal."

"Oh, they doesn't. Not all the time. Just if they feel like it. Or if they know a friend will come by and look for their symbol. If I jump a train to Chicago and back, I don't put no signature nowhere. But I do keep an eye out for my buddies' monicas. Even if it was a mark from last year, I'm always glad to see where they was."

Larry studied the fish scratched in the dirt. "So if you did leave your symbol, how would anyone know whether it was from now or from last year? I mean, if it was painted or something?"

"They wouldn't. Less'n it was on something they knew was blank before. Or if I put on the date. People write the date if they really want people to know what they did and when."

"Makes sense," Uncle Aaron said.

"By the way." Old Fish looked back toward the thread of smoke spiraling from the fire pit. "I'd ask you all to stay for dinner. But there isn't much of it. Just put two cans of soup on the fire."

"Oh, that's okay," Uncle Aaron said. "It's nice of you to think of us."

"No bugs today," Old Fish added. "Just soup."

"But we didn't come to eat your food," Uncle Aaron finished.

The old man waved his hand. "When you live on the road, you give and you take. When you have extra, you give."

The man's eyes rested on something behind my head, and I saw him focus for a minute, as if he was emerging from a trance.

"Ya know," he said. "I remember something now that you ask." He got up and moved to the brush at the side of the packed dirt area, where the buckets lay on their sides like hobo dresser drawers. I wondered if the clothes inside stayed dry in heavy rain. He reached into one and came back with a red handkerchief.

"I think maybe Crumb Boss did run into a doctor awhile back. I was out in Toledo last fall, but it seems like he said a doctor came through then."

"He did?" I jumped to my feet in my excitement. "Is Crumb Boss still here, or did he leave?"

"He isn't here today," Old Fish said. "But I think he might be back tomorrow. Hopped a train to South Bend to visit someone and probably will hop on back tonight. This is all his stuff, so he must be coming back." He motioned with the handkerchief to the bucket on its side.

"Do you remember anything he said about the doctor?" Uncle Aaron asked.

Yes, I thought. *We have to get everything out of him that we can. Who knows if the other hobo will actually come back. Who knows if we'll ever be able to find Old Fish again if we lose him.*

"Oh, I suppose I remember a few things."

"Like what?" Larry asked.

"Tell you what," Uncle Aaron said. "Would you go with us to Rocky's Riverside Restaurant for lunch? We could talk there out of the rain. You're probably used to being out in the rain, but we aren't."

Uncle Aaron made it sound like it would be a favor to us if we moved the conversation to a restaurant.

"Wall, I s'pose it would be a little hard on ya'll to get wet." Old Fish's eyes expanded with interest. "Lemme set this food to the side of the fire and grab my pillowcase."

I didn't care who he thought was getting the best end of the deal. I knew I was, if we were really about to hear something about Dr. Jefferson.

CHAPTER FOUR

Rocky's Riverside Restaurant

I hadn't noticed any foul odors while sitting close to Old Fish in the Hobo Jungle. Now, with all five of us in Uncle Aaron's Camaro, it was a different story. He smelled exactly like Raspy. Amazing. He clutched a stained pillowcase on his knees. I had seen him stuff a comb and toothbrush into it, so I assumed it was his suitcase.

"Why not find a restaurant here in Elkhart?" Terry asked, as if he too was struggling to breathe under the current conditions. "It would be closer."

"Oh, well, we could have!" Uncle Aaron said. "But now we're halfway back to Stratford."

"It's okay." Terry's voice sounded a little constrained, like he was pretty proud of himself for not complaining about the smell. "It's not too far."

"Yeah, I'm sure there's something closer." Uncle Aaron took a right turn toward our small hometown. "But I've been wanting to try out your little village restaurant."

None of us really cared. It would be fun to go wherever our uncle took us. Going with Old Fish may or may not be a benefit, but if he told us anything about Dr. Jefferson, he would definitely earn his meal in my opinion.

We passed the turn-off for Dean's apartment. All three of us boys glanced that way, but saw no one. The Camaro rumbled over the Lexington Street bridge. Instead of turning down Brady Street like normal, we kept going and turned onto Main Street. We passed the library and the grocery store and crossed the river on the bridge with the lampposts and flags. We passed the ice cream shop and pulled up to Rocky's Riverside Restaurant close to Dad's boat motor repair shop.

"Terry, run over and see if your dad has time to join us," Uncle Aaron said.

With relief, we tumbled out of the car. We would now have to sit with Old Fish at a table in an enclosed building. But I remembered Mom's coaching and determined to make no complaint. Terry made a dash for Dad's shop.

"Four of you?" The woman at the front of the restaurant was covered in thick makeup. She wore a severe gray apron the color of the rainy sky, smeared with patches of unidentifiable food items. It billowed around her like a cloud.

"Five, actually, ma'am," Uncle Aaron said. "Maybe six. Would you have a telephone handy since we need to make a quick call to let their mom know we are eating lunch here?"

The woman said nothing but sighed deeply as if this were the worst question she had ever heard in her life. She snatched up five paper menus then pointed to a rotary phone behind the bakery case along the front of the store.

"Thanks," Uncle Aaron said. "Want me to call?"

We nodded wordlessly. Neither Larry nor I wanted to risk crossing the woman by being behind her counter. Old Fish lumbered off to the bathroom immediately, clutching the pillowcase.

The two of us sat where the woman told us to sit and made no complaints or noise until she was gone. A small candle burned cheerfully on the table, as if to make up for the waitress's unwelcoming attitude. Terry burst into the restaurant and sank into a seat beside us, panting.

"Is he coming?" I asked.

He shook his head no. "He's pretty busy. He didn't know if he would make it home for lunch. But guess who I saw out there! Dean!"

"What?" Larry and I asked at the same time.

Terry explained that he had found Dean walking along the road between Dad's shop and the restaurant. He had asked him to join us, but Dean had turned and walked away.

"Who do you think is lying?" I asked. "I don't know if Dean was lying, because if Old Fish knows Buckle, then he is a hobo, like Dean said."

"Where is Old Fish?" Terry asked.

Larry nodded toward the bathroom door where Old Fish had

disappeared. "Do you think he ever takes a bath?"

"Who?" Terry asked, which was the dumbest thing anyone had said all day. Of course Larry meant Old Fish.

"How often do you think he gets to use a toilet?" I asked. "That's what I'm wondering. That would be miserable."

Uncle Aaron returned and slid into a chair. "I bet your parents are going to have a date without you underfoot," he teased. "She didn't sound sad. Said she might take your dad a picnic lunch since he doesn't know if he can go back to the house."

We told Uncle Aaron that Terry had seen Dean. We had just finished that conversation when Old Fish came back looking and smelling much the same as before , with a little soap smell mixed in. Along with the pillowcase, he carried his hat. The hair that had been covered by the hat stuck in every direction like a tangle of underbrush.

"Well, let's all order something and then you can tell us what you know," Uncle Aaron suggested. "Are the cheeseburgers good here?"

"We don't come much," Terry said. "But the food has always been good when we do."

We all ordered cheeseburgers and fries and cokes. The waitress took our order without muttering more than a couple of words.

"Oh, I'll take a coffee too," Uncle Aaron said as she was walking away.

"You want coffee and coke?" she asked, glaring back at him. Her hair was pulled so tightly into a ponytail it looked like she was about ready to scalp herself.

"Yes, please."

"Coffee and coke? Both for you? You want two drinks?"

"Yes, if that's possible. Thanks."

The waitress shook her head and turned away with another sigh.

Uncle Aaron's face broke into a wide grin. "Well, if I didn't know it before, I know it now. Ordering two drinks is not socially acceptable in Stratford."

"I don't know what's wrong with her," Terry said. "She looks like she ate something poisonous and is slowly dying."

This was exceptionally poetic for Terry, and we all laughed quietly.

"I think she's trying to cover up a bruise with that makeup," I said. "I wonder if someone hit her. I saw something purple under all the brown. Also, there's something about her voice that gives me this weird feeling that I've met her before."

"No surprise that someone wanted to hit her," Terry said.

"Do you have any friendly people in this town?" Uncle Aaron glanced toward the front counter where the waitress had disappeared. "Our morning expedition hasn't convinced me."

"Old Fish is nice!" Larry grinned at the hobo. "And you should meet Penny. She's the nicest librarian ever."

"Old Fish is from Elkhart, not from Stratford." Uncle Aaron unrolled his silverware from a paper napkin. "I said *this* town."

"Old Fish is from the road." Old Fish laughed as he said this. "No place he calls home."

But I wanted to focus on the business at hand, not on whether or not we had nice people in our town.

"Old Fish," I said as respectfully as you can call someone *Old Fish,* "what do you remember about the doctor? Did you see him at all?"

"Nope, didn't see him. I'se in Toledo, but Crumb Boss talked about him."

"What did he say?"

"Ah, yes. What did he say? Well, Crumb Boss always has a little chip on his shoulder. Kinda like he's a little better'n the rest of us, so I take what he says with a grain o' salt. I don't know for sure if he ever even saw a doctor or if he made the story up because it sounded fun."

"Oh." My heart sank to my toes. I was so sick of dead ends. How could he tell us that he knew something about the doctor and then say he thought it might all be lies?

The gray apron of the waitress circled back with the cokes. She thumped them heavily on the table, drops of brown liquid jumping out of several of the glasses. She followed this with a small cream-colored mug and poured Uncle Aaron's coffee into it from a carafe.

By the time she had this done, Terry and Old Fish were both finishing up their first glasses of coke. She stared at their empty cups for a moment before snatching them both up.

"Does it matter if these get mixed up?" she asked.

A stunned silence followed as we all stared at her. Who ever heard of a waitress who didn't keep track of who the cups belonged to?

"I don't need another quite yet," Terry said.

"I'll bring a pitcher." She set down the glasses with another sigh.

"So, let's lay aside whether Crumb Boss was lying or not," Uncle Aaron suggested. "Let's assume he was telling the truth. What did he tell you about a doctor visiting?"

"Well. Crumb Boss is full of colorful stories too," he said. "Maybe he was telling the truth, but maybe he embellished the real story a lot too."

"Like what?" Larry asked.

We all would have been happy to hear an embellished story by that point. Even a false story would have been better than this.

"Well, like the red beets," Old Fish said. "He claims that he went to three houses in town one night and all they offered him at every single place was boiled red beets."

"You mean the doctor said this?" I asked.

"No, no, Crumb Boss, hisself. I reckon the doctor maybe had enough money to go buy food. Don't know. Never met him."

I groaned internally and looked up at Uncle Aaron hoping for encouragement. But he didn't even look my way.

"Don't you remember any stories at all about the doctor?" Terry asked.

This was worse. I wasn't surprised that Terry was getting irritated, but his voice sounded so angry I was afraid we would get on Old Fish's bad side and definitely wouldn't get anywhere.

Thankfully, the conversation was interrupted by five plates of fries and cheeseburgers. Boy, did those look good.

"Could we have ketchup, please?" Terry asked.

The waitress scowled and hustled over to the counter. Only a few other people were eating at the restaurant, so I wasn't sure why she was so irritated by his request. She picked up the ketchup bottle and began to shake it vigorously as if she had her hands on Terry himself.

Unfortunately, whoever had the bottle before her had not fastened the lid. Ketchup shot out of the glass neck and arced through the air, splattering on a ceiling light shade. Some of it shot on past the light and landed on the arm of a construction worker who was knifing into a plate of pancakes.

I wanted to laugh, but Uncle Aaron grabbed a stack of napkins and went to work cleaning off the ceiling fan. Just then, a band of firefighters walked in and sat down.

A wave of sadness pushed away my humor. Firefighting. The job I would never do. But I shook myself and focused on the current catastrophe. Uncle Aaron was still mopping ketchup off the light shade.

Thankfully, the construction worker laughed, wiped the ketchup off his arm with a napkin, and kept eating pancakes. In the end, Terry got his ketchup. Uncle Aaron thanked God for the food, and we all dug in. Terry lifted the top piece of bread off his sandwich and picked up the ketchup bottle with the other hand. When I saw the bottle hanging frozen like something in outer space, I looked up at Terry's face. He was staring at his sandwich.

He pointed. "A butterfly."

The rest of us craned our necks to look at his sandwich. Sure enough, in a fold of the lettuce on top of the sandwich, lay a white butterfly. It was nearly hidden, but once you saw it there was no unseeing it.

"Amazing," Uncle Aaron said. "Well, the good thing is that must mean it's fresh lettuce. No one noticed it to pick it out. Let's show it to the waitress and see if she'll replace it."

"Give it to me!" Old Fish said with a chuckle. "Butterflies are my favorite!"

"S-s-sure." Terry picked up the piece of lettuce and passed it over.

I didn't watch Old Fish put the lettuce piece in his mouth, and I tried to mentally close my ears so I wouldn't accidentally hear butterfly wings crunching. But Old Fish could put away food fast, and it wasn't long before he pushed back his plate with nothing left on it but the paper sandwich wrapper.

"Any stories of the doctor that come to mind?" I asked it, even though I no longer believed that he had any memories.

"He didn't talk much. Crumb Boss said he just sat there and stared at the stars."

"Really?"

"Yup. That's about all I remember. He lost something, and I think he told Crumb Boss to look for it. But he'll be back tomorrow, and you can ask him yourself."

"Okay, great, we'll do that," Uncle Aaron said. "Well, I'm fed up. I say we leave before we annoy the waitress more. Should we come to the same place again tomorrow?"

"Yup. Here, take this with you." Old Fish pulled the red handkerchief from his pocket and tossed it onto his plate. "It belongs to Crumb Boss, and everyone knows it. Show that and they'll know who you're looking for even if he's not there."

"Couldn't we ask for him by name?" Uncle Aaron said.

"No, no, take this. Some people don't keep track of names, but they know things like this."

"Um, it's smoking," Larry said.

I looked at Larry. Just last week we had burned a hole in our tent. Was his mind addled from that? But then I saw it too. Old Fish's paper sandwich wrapper had settled over the candle on the table and now burst into flames. The handkerchief was smoking as well.

"Fire!" Terry yelled, leaping to his feet and upending the pitcher of coke over the blaze.

Every conversation in the restaurant stopped and every eye turned toward Terry, who stood above the candle waving the pitcher. The firefighters across the room looked mildly interested but didn't get up. The waitress huffed over, sighing deeper than before when she saw the coke dripping off the table onto the floor. I felt a cold wetness soaking into my jeans.

"I think it's out now," Uncle Aaron said. "If you have a couple of towels, we'll clean this up for you."

"No," she snapped. "I'll get it. Are you ready for the bill?"

A few minutes later, we were packed in Uncle Aaron's Camaro again.

"I hope you didn't leave her a tip," Terry complained. "She

was the worst waitress ever."

Uncle Aaron didn't answer for a moment. The wheels of the Camaro crunched on the gravel as we backed away from the restaurant.

"Here's a long-suffering lesson for you." Uncle Aaron turned the car toward the road. "One of the best ways to show kindness is to leave a big tip even when you get bad service. Most people who deliver bad service are having a bad day, and they expect to get low tips on top of all the trouble they are already having. Giving a big tip shows that someone cares. I would say that counts as long-suffering."

"So you left a big tip?" Larry asked.

Uncle Aaron nodded, and it appeared that we were not going to know more.

"Besides." He glanced at Terry in the rearview mirror. "We left a mess. Maybe we're about to get arrested. Look at this!"

Three police cars, lights flashing, pulled into Rocky's Riverside Restaurant.

CHAPTER FIVE

The Boy with the Box

Uncle Aaron pulled to the side of the parking lot as the police cars drove in. We watched as police officers jumped out and strode for the restaurant.

"They're looking for someone." Old Fish said, chuckling. "Glad it's not me! I seen enough of them in my day."

"Maybe they're looking for that lady we heard about on the radio," I said. "I would think it was the waitress, but she didn't have a tattoo. Oh wait! Maybe that was a tattoo!"

Larry stared at me. "Right! She had something on her face that looked like a bruise, but it might have been a tattoo all covered up!"

"Well, it's none of our business. You all need to go home and change, and I need to take Old Fish back."

"Look, there's Dean again!" Terry pointed to several bushes

on the far side of the restaurant. We could see the black hood among the bushes. As we watched, Dean turned and began running the opposite direction, toward his home.

"I take it he doesn't like police officers." Uncle Aaron shook his head. "Poor boy."

I was not happy when we got home. Partly because, in addition to the damp day, I was now soaked with Coke. Partly because we had gotten almost nowhere in our search and Dean was refusing to help us. And partly, I realized as I slouched on the front porch, because of those firefighters.

They had reminded me.

If I had any dream as a young boy, it was to be a firefighter. In fact, all three of us wanted to be firefighters. It seemed like the perfect combination of excitement, adventure, and compassion. We planned to rescue trapped people and douse flames from huge buildings and generally save the day.

Then, at seven years of age, I lost my leg. The firefighter dream died.

Terry and Larry had gone in to get changed and talk to Mom, but I sat dismally on one white wicker chair with my feet propped on the other one, staring at the garden across Brady Street. I was still there when Uncle Aaron's Camaro pulled in after dropping off Old Fish.

Get yourself together, I told myself. *No use moping.*

I straightened my shoulders and pulled my feet off the chair. Uncle Aaron came up the porch steps, rubbing his back. He sank in the chair across from me.

"I guess we pick up the trail tomorrow," he said. "And let's hope Crumb Boss remembers more than Old Fish."

I nodded.

"I have to go to the chiropractor this afternoon anyway." He rubbed his back again.

"Oh, right."

"Doing okay, Gary?" Uncle Aaron turned his chair so it faced the railing which faced the Number Ten house and Tina's house.

I jumped a little. How had he read my mind?

"Um..."

"Never mind, wrong question." He raised both feet and propped them on the top of the railing, winced a little and then leaned back in the chair. "You are not doing okay. Tell me what's bothering you."

I shook my head again, embarrassed. It was so stupid.

"Those firefighters reminded me about how I used to—" I broke off. It really was such a dumb thing.

"You used to have plans about being a firefighter?"

I looked at him. "Yeah. How did you know?"

He shrugged and looked mysterious. Then he leaned his head all the way back onto the back of the chair. He studied the ceiling of the porch for a while.

"We just painted that."

"I see that. Think I can still smell it a little. Was painting the porch a punishment by chance?"

I laughed again. At least having Uncle Aaron around kept life interesting. How did he know everything?

"Yeah. After the tunnel thing."

Silence settled over us again. I couldn't tell if Uncle Aaron was still thinking about my problem or had given up on me because I was such a complainer.

"You know, Gary, no one's life goes as planned."

Yep, he's still thinking about my problem.

"Let's say that being a concrete worker was the dream job I've wanted to do my whole life. It wasn't, but just imagine. Now I've hurt my back and depending on the outcome, I might not be able to continue in this line of work. I could be crushed. Or I could think, hmmm. Maybe God has something different for me. Maybe something better. Maybe harder. Maybe more important. You know?"

He clapped his left hand down on my left shoulder and gave it a squeeze. I felt much better.

"Have you thought of what else you might do with your life?" he asked. "I know you wanted to be a firefighter. But maybe God has something in mind for you that fits with your skills. Anyone with a strong back and good training can be a firefighter. You have other talents too."

"I haven't thought of anything else. I like drawing and making lists. And numbers and experiments. But usually it's Terry doing the gymnastics, and Larry and I doing the research and recordkeeping."

"Not being the gymnastics guy isn't all bad. You do a lot of note-taking in general, don't you? I keep seeing that notebook around."

"This one?" I pulled it from my pocket. "I'm about to make a list of your advice."

"Ah, well. Never mind. You've got time to know what you should do with your life. But remember. No one's life ever goes exactly like they planned, whether they lose their leg or not." Uncle Aaron laughed and shook his head like he was remembering something. "You won't believe what I wanted to be."

"What?"

"A circus performer. A clown or something."

"No!"

"I am not joking. I even learned to juggle while playing the harmonica."

"Are you serious?" I sat up in my chair and stared at him. I had heard Uncle Aaron playing the harmonica, but I had never seen him juggle. "Why haven't I ever seen that? You've got to show us!"

Uncle Aaron laughed again. "I guess I could now. After I gave my life to the Lord I kind of left it in the past. But sure, I'll juggle for you tonight. By the way, hang on to this handkerchief. Old Fish made sure I kept it when I dropped him off."

Mom, Terry, and Larry all came through the front door and joined us on the porch. Larry had changed out of his Coke-soaked jeans.

Terry hopped onto the porch railing, and Larry and Mom sat on the swing.

"Mom, did you know Uncle Aaron can juggle?" I asked.

"What?" my brothers said together.

Uncle Aaron waved them away. "Tonight, tonight. Not now."

Mom laughed. "Of course I knew that. He was quite a performer. Maybe because his sisters spoiled him. I'm glad he didn't end up traveling with a circus."

"No one spoiled me," Uncle Aaron said. "I'm still as good as new."

"Okay." Mom's voice sounded like a traffic controller about to head our conversation a different direction. This was scary. Was she going to remind us about the long-suffering project? "We have several things that need to be done. I'm sure you had an exciting morning and I want to hear about everything, but it will have to be this evening. Aaron is going to the chiropractor and likely needs a little time alone after all the excitement of the morning."

"Oh, he's doing better than ever!" Terry said from the railing.

Mom went right on. "Dad needs help at the shop this afternoon. You know he said he has a bunch of boats that need to be tuned up before the weekend. Terry, you will go help him. Larry says he wants to go to the library for a book about hobo codes, but I also need someone to make us some cookies. Gary, what would you rather do? Library or making cookies?"

"Library," I said. I didn't exactly excel in the kitchen, and Larry did.

"Okay." Larry shrugged. "I like making cookies. I guess I can trust you to pick out a good book."

"I'll ask Penny if I get stuck," I said. "Good idea. I hope they have a book like that."

"Okay, sounds good," Mom said. "Everyone off to their job. I'm going over to the garden to pull weeds. Anyone is welcome to come help me when they finish their other job."

"Wait." Terry raised a cautious hand. "Welcome to? Or required to?"

Mom laughed. "You don't have to. Oh, that reminds me! We completely forgot to talk about the fruit of the Spirit for this week!"

"Told you so," I said.

"Oh well," Terry sighed. "At least we have a system in place now. All we have to do is come up with an example of someone showing long-suffering, right? And a couple of Bible verses?"

"And a symbol of long-suffering," Larry said. "Gary, draw a picture of Terry. Long and suffering."

Mom waved that idea away without asking for an explanation, and we all went off to our assignments.

When Terry and I headed out the back door, Larry was thumping sticks of butter into a bowl and measuring white sugar.

"What kind of cookies are you making?" I asked.

"Chocolate with peanut butter chips, of course."

Everyone liked them, especially fresh out of the oven. It was the official cookie of our household.

"Let's get moving, Terry," I said. "I want to be back before the cookies cool off."

I drove *Big Ben*, our motorboat, to the library, dropping Terry off at Dad's boat motor repair shop on the way. I looked at Rocky's Riverside Restaurant with new eyes as I passed below it. The police cars were gone. Who had they arrested? The waitress? And why did I feel like I had met her before?

At the library, Penny helped me find a book about hobos with a chart of the hobo writing code in it. Book in hand, I headed back to the dock behind the ice cream shop.

To my amazement, I found Dean on the dock, hidden inside his hood, staring at *Big Ben*. He was holding a cardboard box.

"Dean!" I called before I could get nervous and run the other way. "Where were you this morning? We missed you."

Dean jumped when I called and slouched off the dock. He passed me and headed toward the ice cream shop. I looked with interest at the box, about two feet long and a foot and a half wide, to see what he was carrying. But there was nothing in it.

"I'm busy."

"We went to the Hobo Jungle, but we couldn't find your uncle."

"He's not there much. He lives in Chicago, but he works at the zoo in Toledo. He's only in Elkhart when he goes back and forth."

"When we went looking for you, your mom said he's a zoo-keeper, not a hobo."

"Well, he's a hobo when he's traveling. She doesn't like that word because of how they grew up." Dean was walking farther

and farther away from me.

"How did they grow up?"

"Never mind."

"Okay. Can you go with us tomorrow to look for him?"

"I'll probably be busy again. Maybe next week."

"Is something wrong, Dean?"

Instead of answering, he walked around the corner of the shop, out of sight.

I should have told him to stop by for cookies.

But I had a feeling he would have turned that down too.

I wished I had asked what Uncle Aaron had asked me. Not *Is something wrong?* I should have asked, *What is wrong?*

Because something was obviously not right.

CHAPTER SIX

Monday Night

"Wait." Terry paused his pencil above the rope he was drawing on a tablet on the floor. "I just realized something. I have no idea what long-suffering is. How am I supposed to find someone who shows it?"

"Well, that sounds like the first assignment of the project." Dad leaned back in his recliner. One of the S-shaped vines on the wallpaper seemed to be sprouting from his head. "Define long-suffering."

"Aw, come on!" Terry said. "Can't I just ask you?"

"Sure." Dad shrugged. "But I'm not going to tell you. I think we have a dictionary in the next room."

"Larry!" Terry rolled onto his back and put his hands around his mouth. "Oh, Larry! Are you close to the dictionary?"

"He is a dictionary," I said, and Uncle Aaron, sitting above me on the couch, burst out laughing.

Larry, in fact, was beside the Merriam-Webster dictionary. He was curled up with the hobo book in the library beside the bookcase. He picked the dictionary off the shelf and slid it to me. I picked it up and smelled the warm, papery dictionary scent, then slid it across the carpet to Terry.

Terry turned the thin pages for a while, mumbling about why the dictionary-makers made the thing so hard to navigate. "Okay. Got it. *Patiently enduring lasting offense or hardship.* What's a lasting offense?"

What a cozy evening! Uncle Aaron lay on the couch, not far from Dad in his recliner. Mom rocked in her chair, Larry read a book, and Terry drew rope on an abandoned piece of newspaper. Well, he had been until he got the dictionary. I was drawing too, practicing my hand at a train inspired by the day's events. I thought of Dean and the stinking apartments, and I felt sad for him. Perhaps we could invite him more often. I wondered what he planned to do with that box.

"It's when someone does something mean to you over and over again," Mom said.

"Old Fish was kind of like a *lasting offense* at lunch time," Larry called from the library. "The way he kept on acting like he knew something about Dr. Jefferson, and then kept on having nothing to say."

"It's time we hear the whole story of your morning," Mom said. "I've caught snatches of it here and there."

"And then Uncle Aaron needs to juggle!" I said. "I can't wait!"

"Are you going to feed us cookies, so we have energy?" Terry asked.

"We just ate supper!" Uncle Aaron said. "I'm fed up!"

Larry paused his reading, one hand limp between the pages of his book. "Why do you always say that about eating?"

"Probably because I haven't thought of anything better to say. And also because it makes people roll their eyes."

"Ever the clown," Mom said without looking at Uncle Aaron. "Even when lying flat on the couch."

We told our parents everything we could remember about the morning. The women at the apartment yelling about taking care of children. The security guard at the train yard. The announcement about the woman the police were looking for with the tattoo on her face. The Hobo Jungle. Rocky's Riverside restaurant with Old Fish, the ketchup explosion, the butterfly, and the fire.

"Really," Mom said. "How could so many bad things happen at one meal? A fire? Terry, did you burn that napkin on purpose?"

Everyone laughed a little, like we all hoped Terry would never think of such a thing but couldn't be totally sure.

"Mom," Terry said. "How could you accuse me unjustly?" But then he laughed too.

"I feel bad for Dean's mom and whoever she was talking to," Mom said. "Taking care of children can be a lot of work, but I feel worse for the child that no one wants. Maybe I should be running a babysitting service instead of a garden."

"Oh, that would be great!" Terry said. "We'd never have to

pull weeds again!"

"You'd have to change diapers," Larry said.

"Much easier than pulling weeds."

Mom went off to the kitchen to make popcorn and collect cookies while Uncle Aaron pulled out his harmonica and three socks rolled into balls. I had seen him play the harmonica before, but this time he fastened the harmonica to a frame around his face so he wouldn't have to hold it with his hands. He began to play, and the socks began to circle through the air in time with the song. When he played fast, he juggled fast. When the music slowed, the sock balls slowed.

"That is magnificent!" Larry yelled. "When are you going to teach us?"

Uncle Aaron laughed and threw the balls at Larry. "Tonight?"

A wild and disastrous juggling lesson kept us occupied for the next half hour, after we all raced to our sock drawers and brought down our own sock balls. None of us could get very far, but Uncle Aaron told us we just needed lots of consistent practice.

Mom finally banned us from practicing after one of the juggling balls knocked a framed picture off the wall. "This looks like a great lesson to do outside tomorrow."

"Aw, come on!" Terry flopped back on the carpet. "We have to find Crumb Boss tomorrow, so we can't have juggling lessons then."

We kept talking about Dr. Jefferson staring at the stars and whether Crumb Boss would have more memories about him.

"Who has that handkerchief?" Terry asked. "We'd better not

lose that thing. Who knows who might accuse us of stealing it."

I pulled the handkerchief from my pocket and spread it on the carpet. "Oh, it has writing on it!"

Larry came to look at it with me. "Is it hobo code?"

I shook my head. It was actually hard to read because the handkerchief had a black design on the red background and the writing was also in black.

"Here's a 1A," I said.

"That sounds like an apartment number." Uncle Aaron leaned closer from the couch, squinting.

Mom nodded, looking down at the handkerchief since we were practically at her feet.

"What does this word say?" I pointed to six or seven letters, all capital, across the handkerchief. "That's an A. N. S."

"Lansing!" Larry said. "That's an L at the beginning. Isn't that a town in Michigan?"

Dad nodded. He too was watching us. "It's maybe an hour from here."

"That must be where Old Fish is from," Terry said.

"Not Old Fish." I looked at him. "Crumb Boss. This handkerchief belongs to Crumb Boss."

"Oh right." Terry threw down his pencil and scooted over to us. "What are those symbols at the top?"

We studied the cloth a little. There was something that looked like a cross, and several more numbers and letters. One was a P or a B, it was hard to say. There was a zero, and another P or B and another zero and an X.

"What was Old Fish saying about Monica?" Larry asked. "I didn't get that."

"Bella." Like Dad, Uncle Aaron called Mom this nickname sometimes. "Did you forget to teach your smart sons the word moniker?"

"What's a moniker, then?" Terry asked.

"You're the one with the dictionary," Mom teased. "But I think it's like a nickname or a name that someone goes by."

"He was saying people write their monikers on trains to show they've been there," Uncle Aaron said. "Maybe in hobo language, a moniker is more often a picture than a word that everyone knows belongs to you."

"Kind of like this handkerchief," I said. "This could be Crumb Boss's moniker?"

Uncle Aaron frowned. "Didn't Old Fish say that Crumb Boss's moniker was a crow?"

"Oh, that's right."

"And Old Fish draws a picture of a fish," Terry said.

"Fascinating." Dad shook his head. "It's like a whole new world. I didn't think there were many hobos anymore."

"I don't think there are nearly as many as there once were," Mom said. "But Elkhart has a big train yard, so I guess there are a few who still end up here."

"That's what Old Fish said." I smoothed out the handkerchief, as if hoping to unearth new information about Dr. Jefferson just by looking at it. "He said there used to be a lot more hobos. I wonder if Buckle will be there tomorrow. Dean said he thinks he's gone."

"What? When?" Terry asked.

"I forgot to tell you! I saw him after the library. He said he's busy and can't go with us."

Everyone stared at me.

"How could you forget important information like that?" Larry demanded from six inches in front of me.

"I don't know." I shook my head. "Too much excitement when I got home. Warm cookies and Uncle Aaron all here at once. Yeah, he said he's too busy and his uncle works at the zoo and probably wasn't at the train yard anyway."

"Busy doing what?"

"He didn't say. He was carrying an empty box and heading for the ice cream shop."

No one said anything, but I was pretty sure we were all thinking the same thing. What was he planning to steal this time?

"Hmmm. That's too bad," Mom said. "Well, you know last week God gave you a great example of peacemaking when Terry invited Dean along for pizza. But it could be that God wants you all to learn long-suffering too."

"That's what I was thinking," Dad said. "We want people to get better immediately and behave and be nice to us. The truth is, if someone has been through tough times, it's often hard for them to get past that and live a normal, productive life. So, try to endure patiently the—what did the dictionary say? Ongoing offense?"

"Lasting offense," Terry said.

"And remember," Mom said. "Even if you don't get much out of Crumb Boss, we have that appointment in Chicago on Thursday with the other doctor. Maybe he'll be able to tell us something."

"Is that this Thursday already?" Dad asked.

Mom nodded. "Today is Monday."

"Wow, I'm sorry I forgot about that. I don't know if I can get away from the shop."

"We'll figure it out," Mom said. "Maybe Aaron will go with us."

"Great idea!" I said. "Uncle Aaron, can you move in with us permanently?"

"Yeah!" Larry added. "Don't ever get married, either. We like you just the way you are."

"You do?" Uncle Aaron asked. "Then let me beat you in a game of checkers and see if you still like me."

CHAPTER SEVEN

Crumb Boss

When I woke up the next morning, everyone else was still asleep. Uncle Aaron was sleeping in Terry's bed, and Terry slept in a sleeping bag on the floor. Larry was above me on the top bunk. I looked at the clock and saw it was 6:10.

I rolled out of bed with anticipation for the day ahead. No, I felt downright hopeful.

1. We had found a trace of Dr. Jefferson.
2. Uncle Aaron had encouraged me during our talk on the porch.
3. I was pretty sure, from my limited view of the edges of the curtains, that it was going to be a nice day.

I slid on my wooden leg and my clothes, stepped carefully around Terry, and let myself out of the room. The day beckoned, and I couldn't wait. I hurried down the stairs and out the front door to sniff the morning air.

The sun was sliding over the trees and houses on the other side of the garden. I heard the blare of a train horn, and I smiled, even though there was no one to smile at. Who could be on that train? Dr. Jefferson? Crumb Boss? Uncle Buckle? The world of the hobos filled a person with questions.

"Gut morning!" Tina called from the sidewalk. "Iss early for you!"

I looked down. There was our neighbor Tina out walking her dog, Fritz.

"Good morning!" I hurried down the steps to say hello to Fritz. "I get up early sometimes. We want to find Dr. Jefferson's trail today."

A week before, we had no trail to Dr. Jefferson. So, even though Old Fish had not seen him, it felt like we were much closer. And Crumb Boss had seen him. All we had to do was find Crumb Boss and maybe the mystery would be over. Or, maybe Dean's Uncle Buckle would be there today, and he would know something about Dr. Jefferson.

"Who zis doctor?"

"He's the doctor that cut off my leg when I had cancer." I rubbed Fritz's head and ears and he smiled happily, then took off to sniff Mom's flowers. I thought of how Uncle Aaron had said that anyone could lose their dream job. Things happened, even to people who hadn't lost a leg. "I wanted to talk to him, but he disappeared. Someone said maybe he came to Elkhart on a freight train, so we are trying to find him."

"Oooooo." Tina pulled Fritz away from the flowers. "Iss he bad man?"

It was almost as if a cloud had gone over the sun. It's not that I felt angry toward Tina. Her question reminded me of reality. Maybe he was a bad man. Why else would a doctor hop a freight train?

"I don't know." Fritz came back to me, and I buried my head in his side. "I hope not. I want to find him and find out."

"Okay, okay, I hope you find. Okay, we must go. Someone iss coming to look at my house. Maybe they buy."

"Oh really? You're going to move away?"

"Maybe. Maybe will turn into a museum with the tunnels. We'll see."

"Oh!" I said. I wanted to hear more about this, but Tina and Fritz were already making their way up the sidewalk.

Mom went all out and made sausage and pancakes for us once everyone woke up. I reported on my talk with Tina and that she was planning to sell her house.

"Interesting," Mom said. "I would miss her if she left. Should I send a lunch with you explorers today?"

We considered. But there was really no reason we should be gone over lunch this time. We told her we would plan to come home to eat.

"I'll make sure there's plenty," she said. "Just in case you bring a couple of hobos with you."

"You never know what's going to happen when you go exploring with these three," Uncle Aaron said, snatching up one more sausage link.

"You don't need to explain it to me," Mom said. "I understand perfectly. I'll get you a thermos of water at least. Ferguson said it's supposed to get really hot today."

A tingle of excitement shuddered through me as Uncle Aaron parked along the side of the road again. Now that we knew the blue tarp was there, we could see it in places between the leafy branches of the trees.

Were any hobos under it today?

It was a little after 9 a.m. I checked my pocket to make sure I had the red handkerchief with me, along with my notebook. Larry had the book of hobo codes, and Terry had one of his ropes with him today.

We took the path of tramped down grass and slowed as we reached the trees. We saw no sign of Old Fish, but several people moved deeper inside the jungle.

We reached the edge of the trees and slowed.

"I wonder if we're supposed to knock?" Uncle Aaron asked.

"Let's go in and find out," Terry said. Before the rest of us could voice an opinion, he ducked under a branch and led the way. Uncle Aaron followed him, then Larry, and then me.

"Good morning!" Uncle Aaron called as soon as we were inside. I knew he didn't want to take anyone by surprise in their own camp.

"Morning!" A couple of voices called back. I stepped around Uncle Aaron to see better.

"Need some food?" a gray-haired man asked. His skin was tanned and leathery, and his hair and beard were long, but neatly combed. Kind of like Old Fish's, but this man looked like he at least tried to take care of himself. He held a plastic fork in his right hand. "We're just starting the Mulligan."

Even though it was warm, he wore several layers. A striped shirt. A zippered vest. An old coat with a fuzzy laydown collar that was matted but not dirty.

I was also amazed that he was the second person to offer us food. I had expected hobos would ask for food, not offer it to us.

"We had breakfast half an hour ago, thank you," said Uncle Aaron.

"What's a Mulligan?" Larry asked.

I sighed. There he went again.

The leather-faced man smiled, and his eyes squinted cheerfully under thick eyebrows. He raised the plastic fork and used it to thoughtfully comb his beard. So that's what it was for? I had assumed it was for eating. But maybe it was for both.

"Mulligan stew. That's what everyone calls it. A little of this and that and anything anyone has. It's good you ain't hungry yet because it's not quite ready. But when it's closer, I'm going to cook up some biscuits too."

"Do you put bugs in it?" Larry asked.

The man with the comb eyed Larry closely. "Have you been talking with Old Fish? No, I don't eat bugs."

"Have a seat," a younger man said. He stepped closer to us and turned buckets over for us to sit on.

"We're actually looking for someone," Uncle Aaron said. "Gary, do you have that—"

I nodded and pulled the red handkerchief out of my pocket.

"Looking for a couple of people, really," Uncle Aaron said. "But first of all, do you know if there is a man who goes by Crumb Boss who owns this handkerchief?"

I looked at the handkerchief and then up at the gray-haired man. His smile had faded. The plastic fork froze in place beneath the man's jaws, and his eyes were on the handkerchief in my hand.

My heart sank. Had Old Fish set us up for trouble?

"I am Crumb Boss." His hand fell to his side, and he slipped the fork into his pants pocket. "Where did you get that handkerchief?"

The young man sat on one of the overturned buckets and rubbed his hands together as if he expected a big fight and couldn't believe his luck.

My mouth felt like wood, and I couldn't put any words together.

"Old Fish gave it to us yesterday so we could find you more easily. I see there would have been no need."

"Where's the locket?"

“I’m sorry?” Uncle Aaron asked.

“The locket that was in the box.”

Uncle Aaron looked at me and my brothers.

“Did you boys see a box?”

“There wasn’t a box.” Terry pointed to the five-gallon bucket in the weeds. “Old Fish just pulled the handkerchief out of there.”

“There was a box.” Crumb Boss walked over to the bucket and picked it up. “It’s still here. It had something in it that I was supposed to return to a friend. When I came back last night, the handkerchief was gone and the box is here empty.” He reached into the bucket and pulled out a smooth wooden box which opened easily on fine metal hinges. He held it sideways to show us that it was empty. “Now you come here showing me the handkerchief, and you say you don’t know where the locket is?”

I swallowed. We were in bad shape.

“I guess I should have stuck with my instinct,” Uncle Aaron said. “I didn’t want to take the handkerchief. I see now it might have been a plot of some kind. I’m very sorry about the loss of the locket, but I assure you we never saw it. Could we help you look in the grass here?”

The gray-haired man eyed Uncle Aaron. “You look like a man who speaks the truth.”

“I am speaking the truth. The three boys were here too. By the way, I’m Aaron. This is my nephew Gary, who is looking for a missing doctor, and his brothers Terry and Larry.”

“Missing doctor?” Crumb Boss dipped into his pocket for the plastic fork and began running it through his beard again.

The young man sighed. Getting off the bucket, he went back to the kettle over the fire pit. No fun times for him this morning.

I looked up at Crumb Boss and thought I saw a twinge of compassion in his eyes. I decided to take the plunge and tell all.

"I had cancer and lost my leg when I was seven." I pulled up my pants leg and showed him the wood that should have been muscle and bone. "I'm trying to find the surgeon who did the surgery to find out more about it, but he disappeared. His name was Dr. Bruce Jefferson, and we think he came here to Elkhart on a freight train. But we don't know when."

"What did he look like?" Crumb Boss asked. Again, my heart sank. He did not know him. Old Fish had been wrong.

"Well, I was pretty young when I saw him last," I said. "But I think he was tall and thin with a black beard. Then. And he wasn't very old, Mom said. Maybe 35-40 now."

Crumb Boss said nothing. Traffic whizzed past on the road behind us. Beside us a train rumbled in toward the train yard.

"I could try to find a picture of him." I raised my voice to be heard above the train noise. "If that would help."

Crumb Boss smiled sadly and ran his thumb across the small wooden box. He was not nearly so happy-go-lucky as Old Fish, but he felt more trustworthy to me.

"No, no. That's fine." He raised his voice too, in a tired way, as if he was used to living around trains and knew how to adjust his volume. "I know him well. He's the one this locket belonged to. I was going to send it to him, but now it's gone."

CHAPTER EIGHT

The Owner of the Locket

"You know him?" I leaned forward.

"We spent a lot of time together when he was here, which was last fall." Crumb Boss nodded. "Sit down, and we'll talk. I'm a bit of a jungle stiff. Always around. Are you out to sue this man or something?"

"Oh no!" I said. "I want to talk to him. And I guess..." my voice trailed off. "I guess I do want to find out what kind of a man he is."

"What's a jungle stiff?" Larry asked.

Crumb Boss laughed quietly. "Old Fish didn't teach you the lingo? A jungle stiff is someone who stays in the jungle mostly and don't travel much no more. Isn't always waiting for the next train to be made up. Stiff just means a person."

"What does it mean to make up a train?" Larry asked.

"Every time a train heads out, it's made up of different cars," he said. "So someone in the office has a list of these cars that are supposed to go on the train to Chicago at 4 pm or 10 pm, or whatever. And they'll line them all up on the same track and then hook them together and then call for the engine or engines that are going to pull them. And finally, the whole thing is ready to go, and it takes off."

I had never thought about how trains were put together.

Uncle Aaron seated himself on a bucket, and the rest of us followed. I had to brush a long-legged spider off my bucket before sitting down.

"Watch out for snakes," Larry whispered to Terry, who is petrified of snakes.

"Not too many around here." Crumb Boss's ears had picked up the whisper. "We keep this area pretty stomped down."

He settled on a bucket himself.

"So, did you say Dr. Jefferson lost this box while he was here?" Uncle Aaron asked.

I was glad he asked because I was confused too.

"He told us to call him Bruce." Crumb Boss picked up a stick and began peeling off the bark. He reached into his pocket for a knife, snapped it open, and whittled as he talked. "Yeah, he had a backpack with all his stuff in it, like we all have. And then he had this second bag with extra things in it, I guess. And one day he and I went on a short hop. We thought the train was stopping, so we went to the door because we wanted to jump out before the train completely stopped. He put the packs down on the floor of the boxcar ready to throw them out, like you do when you want to get off. And I wasn't paying good attention and knocked my foot against his second pack and away it went over the edge. I still thought it would be fine, and we could go back for it. But then the train sped up instead. We were farther away from the next rail yard than I thought.

"Wait, what?" Terry asked. "You throw your pack out before you jump?"

Crumb Boss nodded and smiled. "Want me to teach you? You'd probably be good at it."

Terry grinned. "Sure!"

"Maybe sometime. But the rule is you never want to jump off a moving train with a pack on. So you throw it off just so and then you jump off too. After it stops, you go back and collect it. Or you leave the pack on the train and jump off and run beside the car and grab your pack. But, anyway, I felt terrible that his pack was missing because I kicked it out. Bruce came and went after that. Finally, he told me he was leaving and might not be back. 'If you ever go there again,' he says, 'and find my pack by chance, you can have the pack and everything in it. Just send me the locket,' he says. It snowed soon after that, and I didn't get down that way for a long time. Not until a few weeks ago when the snow melted. And I had to pad my hoof a long ways to get there too."

"What do you mean, pad your hoof?" Larry asked.

"Walk." Crumb Boss laughed. He didn't seem to mind Larry's constant questions. "I was sure it was lost or someone else took it. But it so happened I remembered the place, and I found it. Slept in a ditch a few nights until I flipped back on for the ride back. And sure enough, the locket was in there and looked great. So I was going to walk over to the post office. I was going to do it today. But now it's gone. I'm too embarrassed to send him the box without the thing inside."

I had listened to this story with some interest and fascination, but also with impatience. I wanted to ask questions. Lots of questions. More than Larry.

"Do you know where he went when he left? When did he leave?"

"Along about Thanksgiving. He went west a ways. Not far west, he said. Just a little west. But I don't know where he'll go next. People on the road, you can't pin them down."

Another train whooshed by. The train noises were so big, like the sound of a vacuum cleaner and a thunderstorm and a machine shop all in one. I wondered if anyone was ever able to get a wink of sleep in the Hobo Jungle. And had Old Fish been right that Dr. Jefferson lay awake, staring at the stars?

"How do you know he was a doctor?" I asked. "You said he told you to call him Bruce."

Crumb Boss nodded and his eyes squinted at something above and behind us as if he could almost picture Dr. Jefferson walking into the Hobo Jungle through the trees.

"He told us he was a doctor. Didn't seem to mind if we knew. But didn't seem to want any officials to know. Some of us called him Doc for a while, but he asked us not to do that. He said it's okay if we know he's a doctor, but he didn't want to go by that name."

My stomach turned again. *Why didn't he want officials to know he was a doctor?*

Crumb Boss went on. "I think he talked to me more than to anyone. Told me some stuff about his life and how he ended up here. Not everything, I suppose, but a little. Said he was tired of being a doctor. Seemed really wore out for such a young man. Like he was almost depressed or something, when he got here. I took him out on rides, taught him a little about the rails, and he relaxed. Wanted to learn all the symbols and code and such. We'd sit here of an evening and write messages in hobo code. Or make up our own symbols for words if we didn't know of a symbol already made. Good times."

Everyone was silent again. Crumb Boss seemed almost sad, like he was talking about a long-lost friend.

"How long was he here?" I asked.

"How long?" Crumb Boss had the plastic fork in his hand again. "Oh, he was good with the Mulligan stew too, as long as Old Fish wasn't around to slip in grasshoppers. But let's see. I think maybe he came at the beginning of summer last year. And stayed until almost Thanksgiving."

"Wow!" Terry said. "He was here all last summer! Too bad Gary didn't know that then or he could have come here to talk to him."

I agreed. But at the same time, I wondered. Would a conversation with a doctor living in the Hobo Jungle actually have made me feel better? Something seemed wrong about the whole thing. Why would he join the hobos if he had nothing to hide?

"Yeah, maybe." Crumb Boss looked at Terry, thoughtfully combing his beard with the fork. "But if he would have heard someone was here looking for a doctor, I bet he would have left. Seemed like there was something in his past that made him not want to talk about practicing medicine much. I told him one time that when I was young, I thought I was going to be a doctor. He looked at me and shook his head and said he thinks I have a good enough life right where I am. Almost like he thought being a hobo was a better career than being a doctor. Can you imagine?"

The fire popped under the pot of Mulligan stew and a flurry of ash ascended into the air like a small tornado.

Looking at the fire made me think about how hot it was already. We were mostly in the shade, but I felt sticky and sweaty. Maybe some of it was from being nervous. I could still barely believe that we were talking to someone who had known Dr. Jefferson for several months. There was a question I wanted to ask, but I couldn't force my mouth to form the words. I asked another one instead.

"Where do you get food for the whole summer?"

"Oh, most hobos have a little money, and they also know how to beg." He laughed. "A lot of hobos ride the trains until their money runs out, and then they get a job somewhere for a while. But there's also food pantries and soup kitchens and stuff around. The food pantries give mostly canned goods, but we'd open a few cans and throw it into the Mulligan stew. You need to try some."

"Do you know Buckle?" Larry asked. "He's our friend's uncle."

"He's not exactly a friend," Terry said.

"Buckle? Yeah, I know Buckle. He comes and goes. Not here today."

"He was here last night," the younger man said from his seat close to the pot of stew.

"Oh, there you go."

"Do you think it's worth trying to find him?" Uncle Aaron asked. "Would he have more information about where Dr. Jefferson may have gone?"

"Oh no," Crumb Boss said. "No way. He didn't talk to Buckle much. Talked to me more than anyone. And I don't even know much."

That made me feel better about not finding Dean's uncle at least. Although it still didn't explain why Dean had abandoned us. I summoned my strength. I had to ask that question.

"Crumb Boss, do you think Dr. Jefferson was a good man?"

He looked at me as if he was not quite sure what the word *good* meant. Maybe I didn't quite know what I meant either.

"I don't know much about what kind of doctor he was." He tapped the fork on his knee, as if he imagined that it was a surgeon's scalpel, ready to cut. "But I reckon he was a better man than a lot of hobos."

He had just said this, when the branches parted and Old Fish lumbered into the clearing, dripping with sweat and breathing hard.

"There you are!" He leaned against the trunk of a small tree and panted for a few seconds. "I just saw Buckle's nephew down by the W yard, so I bet Buckle is down there too! I knew you wanted to find him, so I hoofed it over here as fast as I could!"

We looked at each other. Dean was here too?

CHAPTER NINE

Buckle's Trail

A branch swung against Old Fish's hat as he leaned down to position a five-gallon bucket to sit on. He let the hat fall into the weeds and sank onto the bucket.

Crumb Boss, Uncle Aaron, Terry, Larry, and I exchanged confused glances. After what Crumb Boss had said, we didn't know if we wanted to talk to Buckle anymore.

"Where did you see him?" Larry asked.

"In the W yard, close to a train that's being made up!" Old Fish said this as if it was the most important thing in the world. Perhaps he could sense that we weren't sure that his information mattered, and he was trying to convince us. "Out on the outside track. I was coming from spending the night in the cemetery. Something everyone should do now and then. Good for deep thoughts."

"He might not be there by the time we go over." I guess I felt a little weary of Dean.

"But I saw something else!" Old Fish paused and licked his lips as if we were about to hear something that would change our lives. "I started checking out the cars on that outside train, and sure enough, there was one with Buckle's monica and today's date. Today is 6-23-87, ain't it? Seems like Old Buckle hisself might be hanging out in that car with his symbol. I can't believe I picked it out!"

Uncle Aaron confirmed that June 23 was the correct date. "What does his moniker look like?"

"Anybody got some writin' paper ?" Old Fish asked. "I'll draw it for you. Too much to draw in the dirt."

Crumb Boss sat listening. I looked at him, wishing he would say something. Couldn't he advise us to go find Buckle? Or advise us not to go find Buckle? Maybe he could tell Old Fish that Buckle was not a good source of information about Dr. Jefferson. But he offered nothing. My hand moved to my pocket, and I slid my notebook out.

I flipped it open to a blank sheet and handed Old Fish my pen.

"Now we're talkin'!" Old Fish put my notebook on his greasy pant leg and began to draw, holding the pen with his fist.

We were silent, watching him turn corners with the pen. When he finally held up the notebook, we gulped in surprise and admiration. Old Fish was a gifted artist! He had drawn a square belt buckle with something that looked like a tree sprouting out of it. Buckle's symbol.

"Did you see Buckle there?" Terry asked. "Shouldn't he have been there when you went by?"

"Train doesn't leave until noon." Old Fish reached into his pocket for his pipe. "He'll be there at the time the train leaves. Probably down in the cemetery eating his lunch in some corner."

Uncle Aaron looked at his watch. "A little before 11 now. Well, boys, how about we see if we can find Buckle? Even just to say hi to him since he's Dean's uncle. Maybe we'll find Dean over there too. What do you think?"

We agreed and thanked Crumb Boss and Old Fish for their help.

"If I think of more questions, can I come back?" I asked Crumb Boss. "Are you usually here at the jungle?"

"I'm a hobo." His eyes squinted in a smile. "I'm never usually anywhere."

"Old Fish!" Larry got up off his bucket with yet another question. "Did you hear if they found the skinny lady with the tattoo on her face? We heard yesterday they were looking for a woman who they thought might be riding the rails."

"Nope. Never heard nothin'. But I don't converse with those men in uniform if I can help it."

"Wait, where's the W yard?" Terry asked. It's good we had Terry with us this time. We liked to joke about him not being very smart, but the truth was he saved us sometimes and this was one of the times. We had no idea where to go.

"W for West." Crumb Boss smoothed the dirt at his feet. "Look here." He drew a long line, then drew a bunch of short

lines for tracks. The short lines veered away from the main line and then reconnected down the track. "We're sitting right beside the receiving yard." He drew more lines in the dirt. "About 15 tracks here. Then they break the trains down, push them over this little hill called the hump, and then direct them to a certain section of the classification yard. Then, once they've got the cars all divided, they send them to either the westbound yard or the eastbound yard. Westbound is the W yard. It's a long walk from here." He pointed with his stick to different sides of his bulge of track. "Got it?"

"They have a car." Old Fish pulled his pipe from his pocket and pointed it toward the road. "They don't have to walk."

"Yes, I think I got it," Uncle Aaron said. "How do I know when I get to the W yard? Is there a sign?"

"Nope," Old Fish said. "But you can tell. You go past that big bulge of seventy tracks like he drew and then there's only seven tracks for going west, so you know you're there. It's on the outside track and that car might be about in the middle of the train."

"Do they really mean NO TRESPASSING?" Larry asked.

Old Fish shrugged and handed my notebook back to me. Crumb Boss shrugged.

"You find out what they mean by how they act." Crumb Boss stood up and wrapped the wooden box in the red handkerchief. "You take this, Gary." He looked me in the eye. "If you find him, tell him I meant to return it, but it got stolen before I had the chance. I was too embarrassed to send the empty box."

"Don't you want your handkerchief?" I asked.

"No, no. This way he'll know for sure it came from me."

Uncle Aaron interceded for me. "Is there a chance someone could accuse Gary of stealing the locket?"

Crumb Boss shook his head. "Why would he steal the valuable and then walk around with an empty box and useless handkerchief that tie him to the crime?"

We walked out silently to Uncle Aaron's car through the blazing sun. A trickle of sweat meandered down my back.

We piled in, with Larry jumping in the front because it was his turn. He passed the jug of water around for each person to have a drink.

"Well, Uncle Aaron, I don't suppose you ever pictured yourself in a Hobo Jungle two weeks ago?" I asked.

"No, not really." Uncle Aaron started the car and opened all the windows. He had air conditioning, but it would take a while to catch up and we were only going on a short drive up to the yards. "But if I've learned anything in life, it's that we should be flexible. If we tell God we'll do whatever He wants us to do, we have to be prepared that this could look really strange. Sorry, Gary. That was a long answer. It's just that I've seen too many people start off on acts of service or missions of some kind, and after a while they give up. Something unexpected came up and they felt like they were in over their heads and couldn't handle it anymore. We need to expect the unexpected and God will be faithful."

"Are you saying you think you're serving God by helping Gary find this doctor?" Terry's tone of voice indicated that he didn't think anything involving me could be serving God.

"Why not?" I snapped.

"Be quiet, Gary," Terry snapped back. "I'm not saying it's not important. It just doesn't seem like missionary work."

"Doesn't have to be traditional mission work to be serving God," Uncle Aaron said. "And, yes, I think I'm serving God now."

"Well, I'm really glad you are helping," I said. "We would be lost without you. Can we drive down the road we went in on yesterday?"

"Good question. I guess like Crumb Boss said, we'll find out."

We drove down the road, past the sign that welcomed us to the Elkhart Train Yard and then warned us of No Trespassing. We passed the block building with the outside stairs that we had ascended the day before.

"There's the hump he was talking about!" Larry yelled from the front. "Wow, that thing is 20 feet high!"

No vehicles darted out to cut us off or pull us over.

"Hopefully there aren't any loose trains in this yard," Larry said. "I read one time—"

"You read too much," Terry said. "And anyway, if a train derails and comes bouncing toward us, Uncle Aaron will dodge it."

"I will?" Uncle Aaron jerked the wheel to the right just enough to flip our stomachs into the air. We all sucked in our breath and then hollered in protest.

"Pass me that water again, will you?" Uncle Aaron said. "Got to keep life interesting. But don't you ever do that when you learn how to drive."

"Or at least not when Mom is with us?" I asked.

"Put it this way." Uncle Aaron took a big gulp of water. "If you do something like that and your mom is along, do not say that Uncle Aaron inspired you. That's all I'm asking of you, Gary."

We all laughed. Uncle Aaron guided us past the classification yard. It wasn't hard to pick out because there were rows and rows of tracks, many of them holding cars. The road bent slightly to the right, and then slightly to the right again as we drove around the bottom of the bulge of seventy tracks.

"Think we're close?" Uncle Aaron slowed the car. "How many tracks do you see?"

"I think this might be it!" Thankfully, I had jumped in on the passenger's side which meant I got the better view. "Oh, right there! It's right there! The buckle!"

Uncle Aaron slammed on the brakes.

"We passed it. See? About four cars back," I said. "Right beside a tanker car."

Uncle Aaron reversed a little, and then we all saw it.

It was a red boxcar with metal ribs running up and down it about every two feet. The doors were open. White numbers and letters had been painted on the car by the manufacturer. Huge graffiti letters had been added by random artists, I supposed. Because of these letters rising nearly halfway up the car, I was surprised I had even seen the buckle on the end of the car.

"Well, let's see, there's a woods up ahead on the left," Uncle

Aaron said. "And it looks like it's outside of the rail yard. I'll park over there, and then we can walk back and check out that boxcar. I'm thinking though, if he isn't there, that we should leave again."

"Right." I watched a railway worker in a reflective vest walk along the line of cars. I heard the rattle of a chain as he made an adjustment and went on. "I don't think he's going to have much to say about Dr. Jefferson anyway, if Crumb Boss is right."

Uncle Aaron drove slowly toward the woods.

"There's Dean!" In the front seat, Larry nearly leaped out of the car, then clapped his hand over his mouth because the windows were open.

"Where?"

"He disappeared behind that car. He's on the other side of this train. But I know it was him. He was carrying a cardboard box."

CHAPTER TEN

The Boxcar

As Uncle Aaron parked the car as much in the shade as possible, we discussed Larry's sighting. Would we have a chance to talk to Dean? And why was he here?

"I wonder if he found out that his uncle would be around and is bringing him supplies," Uncle Aaron suggested. "You would bring me supplies if I wanted to catch a train, wouldn't you?"

"If you took me along." Terry led the way across the road toward the rail yard. "Hey, why not? Wouldn't that be a blast? Jump on a train and eat supper in Chicago tonight? We could call Mom and tell her we'll be a little late."

I wasn't really into the banter because I was trying to think through why Dean would be here without us.

1. He had told us that we should meet his uncle.
2. He had said he was too busy to go with us after all.
3. Now, here he was. If he was just meeting his uncle, why wouldn't he have told us to join him?

"We'll probably run into Dean when we go find Buckle," I said. "I guess then we'll find out what's up. I hope."

"Careful what you wish for," Uncle Aaron teased me.

We crossed the road we had driven up and stepped onto the crushed rock beside the track. We walked along the length of the train toward the boxcar with the buckle. We couldn't see the symbol from here, but I was pretty sure I knew which car it was. It was a little farther than I had expected.

Walking beside the cars intimidated me. The cars towered above us. They also seemed twice as long as they had appeared from the road. Perhaps they would have seemed shorter if it had been cooler.

I found something poetic about the train yard, though. The square wooden railroad ties buried in the black rock. The metal spikes and brackets that held everything in place. The dead leaves from last fall lying in between the ties, mingling with the rock.

Where had these cars been before? The graffiti and paintings told part of their story, but not all. Possibly every car had traveled from the East Coast to the West Coast.

We weren't far from the boxcar when Dean stepped out in front of us between two cars. He was empty-handed.

"What's up?" He spoke from deep inside the black hood. It was unbelievable that he could wear that thing on such a hot day.

"Hey, there you are!" Terry said. "We thought you were busy. We finally heard from someone else that your uncle might be close by because they saw his symbol."

"Yeah, he's here somewhere." Dean looked down the line of cars. "You know his buckle symbol?"

"We saw it."

"Okay, yeah, I saw it too. A few cars up. I haven't gotten to check on him yet. Want me to show you? It's pretty cool to see inside a boxcar. And we can check to see if his pack is in there. If it is, it means he'll be along shortly."

"Will we get arrested for climbing into the car?" I asked.

"Who's going to arrest you?" Dean was already leading the way. Terry set off with him and Larry followed them. Uncle Aaron and I came last and dropped behind far enough that I could whisper my complaint to him.

When we were far enough away, I said, "I don't get it. Why couldn't we have come along with him? This would have been perfect."

"Remember what I was saying a little earlier," Uncle Aaron said. "Unexpected things happen. Maybe we need to practice long-suffering."

"Oh, you're just like Mom!" Terry protested from ahead. Apparently, we had not been as quiet as we thought. "Always tying that project in with everything."

"Well, she's my sister." Uncle Aaron shrugged as if it was a sad situation he could do nothing about. But we knew he liked Mom a lot.

"Here we are!" Terry pointed to the spray-painted buckle now right in front of us. "Now let's see if we can get in this thing."

"Easy." Dean put his hands on the floor of the box car and jumped inside. Terry followed. Uncle Aaron scrambled up next and gave both Larry and me a hand since we were the shortest.

We were all inside the car in thirty seconds, our eyes adjusting to the dimness.

"Uncle Buckle, you here?" Dean asked.

There was no answer.

"What time is it?" I asked. I had heard a hissing noise that reminded me of one time when I had heard brakes releasing on a bus right before it took off.

"Well, if I could see I could tell you," Uncle Aaron said. "But if you're worried that it's noon, don't be. It's not. I'm guessing it's a little after eleven."

"He always puts his pack on that end," Dean said, pointing to the east end of the car. "Check for a bag and we'll know he's coming back soon. I just remembered something I need to grab off my bike for him. Be right back."

Dean jumped out and disappeared from view.

"Larry, why don't you have your flashlight along when we need it?" Terry grumbled. "I have my rope."

"Oh!" Larry reached into his pocket. "I do have it. Never thought of it."

I reached into my own pocket. Alongside my notebook I felt

the smoothness of the wooden box and the coarse red handkerchief. I sure hoped that thing wouldn't get us in trouble. If we were accused of trespassing, would we be searched and asked to give an account for everything we had with us? How would I explain the empty box? I was still leery about it. Maybe I should have left it in the car just in case. But the car could be searched too.

Larry's flashlight lit up the dim corners of the boxcar. A pile of thick cardboard and a small bag sat in one corner.

"There's a bag!" Terry said. "Must be his."

Sque-e-e-e-eak.

We all turned.

What was that? The boxcar door nearest to us rolled closed. My heart sank. Someone from the railroad was checking the cars, and we were about to get into trouble. Then, I saw Dean's form outlined in the half-opened door. He didn't say anything, and I couldn't see his face. But he dashed across the opening and then the other door rolled shut, crashing against the first one.

We were plunged into complete darkness except for the beam of Larry's light.

"What in the world is going on? Shine the light that way, Larry." Terry leaped toward the door, but we heard the soft click of a latch before he got there. By the light of the flashlight, I saw Terry raise his fist to bang on the door.

"Just wait," Uncle Aaron said, right behind Terry. "I wouldn't make any noise."

"Why not?"

"If Dean locked us in as a mean trick, it won't help to pound. But maybe something else is going on. Maybe he's trying to keep us from getting noticed by the railroad crew. If that's the case, we may as well play along and stay quiet."

"Or possibly," Terry said, "he's still trying to get even with us, and this is the best way he could think of to bury us alive."

CHAPTER ELEVEN

Art on the Floor

When Dean's father slammed the basement door on us a few weeks before and trapped us in the tunnel under Tina's house, I had been pretty terrified. But I hadn't been entirely surprised. Something had seemed off about Harold's "antique dealer" disguise and voice.

But this time, on this hot June day, I stood in the boxcar completely stunned and confused. What was going on? What had gone wrong? Or was Dean playing a little trick on us and about to open the door again?

We gathered on the inside of the boxcar door, in a hot, sweaty group. Uncle Aaron took the flashlight from Larry and held it above us so that we could all see each other. Our noses and heads cast weird shadows across our bodies and on the floor. A train horn blared in the distance, and closer to us I heard the *ding-ding-ding* of a bell. I saw a streak of rust on the boxcar floor, and I remembered Larry's story about people starving to death in boxcars that get shunted into empty buildings.

This car is made of metal. The thought popped into my mind like a bad headache. *Not stone that you can dig through. Not wood that you can carve. Metal.*

"Well." Uncle Aaron cleared his throat as if he needed more time to prepare his words. "Shall we take a vote? Who thinks Dean did this on purpose to be mean?"

I wasn't sure what I was expecting, but when all four of our hands raised into the shadowy air, I felt the headache sensation spread through my entire body. Even though none of us knew for sure, the fact that we were all suspecting Dean of treachery seemed to make it true.

I looked down at the streak of rust again, and I thought of something else. We wouldn't die of starvation. Not a chance. No, we would die of thirst.

"Did anyone bring the water bottle?" I asked.

No one had.

"It was almost empty anyway," Uncle Aaron said. "If that makes you feel any better."

We laughed shakily, and all felt better. If a person could still laugh, there was life and hope.

"Gary." Uncle Aaron swung the flashlight directly on me. "Here's where we need your list expertise."

"Okay?" I pulled my notebook and pen from my pocket.

He laughed. "I wasn't actually thinking you would write the

list down, but sure, why not. Let's think of a list of at least three things we're thankful for. Then we can start thinking about what to do next."

"Are you sure we shouldn't pound on the door?" Terry asked.

Uncle Aaron considered this, swinging the light on Terry.

"I guess maybe we could. Although I think there's a good chance Dean will let us back out and laugh about it being a joke."

Terry's eyes widened. "You're right. I don't want him to get the pleasure of listening to me pounding."

"We still have forty minutes until the train leaves at noon," Uncle Aaron said, switching the beam to his watch. "Let's say if he doesn't open the door in ten minutes, we start pounding."

We all agreed that this was a good plan. I sat on the boxcar floor close to the streak of rust and readied my pen for the list.

"I'm glad I'm not in here alone," Larry said.

"Right." Terry's shoes shifted not far from me. "And I'm glad Uncle Aaron is along."

"Right!" I said. "And I'm glad that Uncle Aaron knows what to do no matter how bad the trouble is."

Uncle Aaron laughed but I think he liked my vote of confidence. I scratched out the list.

1. We aren't here by ourselves.
2. Uncle Aaron is with us.
3. Uncle Aaron knows what to do no matter what happens.

I circled the list with a flourish, my pen making a thin, dancing shadow in the flashlight's beam.

"I feel better already!" Larry said.

"Me too." I put the pen back in my pocket. "By the way, this floor is still a little cooler than the air. You should all sit down."

Feet and legs rearranged in the light as everyone joined me on the floor.

"So, this is what a first-class hobo ticket feels like," Uncle Aaron said. "Okay, what do hobos do while riding? How do you want to pass the next few minutes until we start pounding?"

"Art!" Larry said. "Does anyone have a marker?"

No one did, but I pulled my pen back out.

"I don't want this thing ruined." I handed it over to Larry.

"Don't worry, don't worry." Larry waved his hand at me. "I'll write out as much of the hobo code as I can remember. Too bad I didn't bring my book along."

Larry switched from sitting cross-legged to lying on his stomach for better access to the boxcar floor. He tested the pen.

"Okay, well, it writes," he said. "Not the best, but it does."

"All right, we are captive students," Uncle Aaron said. "Teach us a lesson, Larry."

"Okay! Well, let's see. I remember this one. See if you can figure it out."

Larry wrote a large capital I and then the number 8.

"I eight?" Terry asked.

As soon as he said it, we all laughed. *I ate.*

"That was what a hobo would write down at a place that had offered him food," Larry said. Next, he drew five slash marks and two horizontal lines through them. "This means *unsafe place.*"

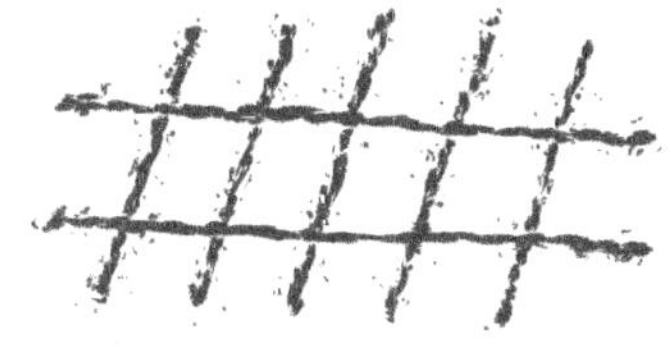

Larry remembered a few more, but he soon ran out of teaching material.

"Hey, we all need a monica!" Terry said. "To leave as a signature that we were here."

"It's *moniker.*" Larry's voice held a little scorn, but I could tell he thought it was a great idea. "Mine will be a flashlight on top of a book. My nickname will be Bright."

"Typical," Terry said. "Your nickname even sounds smart."

"That's not what I meant! I'm not saying I'm smart. I'm saying I have a light."

"Yeah, yeah, yeah. Okay, my monica—" Terry emphasized the ending of his version of the word—"will be a rope with a knot in it."

"And you'll go by Old Knotty?" Uncle Aaron asked.

Larry drew his symbol, then passed the pen to Terry, who drew his knot. Uncle Aaron got me to do his. He said he would take a fish and call himself Young Fish. I added my own, a notebook and pen, and called myself List Boss. The monikers formed a rough circle, and Larry added the date to the middle. June 23, 1987.

"Well, that was fun," Terry said, lying back on the boxcar floor. "When Dean finally opens the door, I'll ask him why he

June 23, 1987

didn't stay and join our game."

"If he opens the door," Uncle Aaron said. "It's been ten minutes, so I'm thinking—"

Exactly as Uncle Aaron said *thinking*, the car lurched. We heard a clank from the front of the car and the back, like connections tightening together.

"What was that?" Terry asked.

The car lurched again, but this time it didn't come to a complete stop. It began moving slowly west.

"That," Uncle Aaron said, "is probably the train leaving Elkhart."

CHAPTER TWELVE

A Strange Squeak

No one said anything. No one except the train, which seemed to be whispering farewell to the Elkhart yard. *Rumble-rumble-rumble, good-bye. Rumble-rumble-rumble, good-bye.*

"Are you sure they're not arranging the cars?" Larry asked. "You know, Crumb Boss was saying how they have that classification yard. The cars all get—"

"Larry, I'm not smart like you are," Terry interrupted. "But even I know that this isn't the classification yard. Old Fish said this is the W yard."

"Besides," Uncle Aaron sighed. "I don't think they would be classifying the train a few minutes before departure time. Although why it's leaving early, I don't know. Let's see, who told us it would leave at noon?"

"Old Fish," I said.

"Yeah, the man who eats butterflies and sleeps in graveyards." Terry's voice held an edge of sarcasm. "Reliable man for sure."

Terry could really manage words when he got upset.

"Well, I don't feel like a reliable man myself." Uncle Aaron was holding the light so I couldn't see his face. "Your mother might put a stop to sending you with me. I don't know why I didn't think about it that Old Fish might not be right on the departure time."

The train shuddered as if it was preparing to jump the track. But it went on, hurtling forward, picking up speed. I remembered the Bible story about the ten plagues and a darkness so thick it could be felt. The darkness in the train car seemed heavy too. Or maybe it was the oppressive heat that weighed me down like a blanket. If only we could see out, perhaps I wouldn't imagine that we were about to hit something every time the train jolted.

I heard an odd squeak like a door on a hinge, but no door opened. I felt a little dizzy. Suddenly, right in the middle of the dizziness, I remembered something that made me so mad at myself I collapsed backwards on the floor. This was the wrong thing to do, of course, because everyone was on edge anyway, and I think they assumed I had fallen back dead. I heard a shuffle of feet and then the flashlight shone like the sun right into my face. I had the feeling my brothers and uncle were both standing over me.

"Gary, what happened?" Uncle Aaron asked. The beam of light shook as if he had gotten the tremors. I felt bad for creating the scene, but I felt even worse about my sudden thought. I sat up and assured the others I was fine.

"I just remembered a lie Dean told when we got on the boxcar. I'm sure it was a lie. It had to be. And if I had noticed it at the time, it would have alerted me to follow him, and we wouldn't be in this mess. Remember how he said he was going to his bike for something for his uncle? There's no way he biked here."

Uncle Aaron repositioned the flashlight so it shone over all of us again.

Terry frowned at me. "I don't see why not. I could bike this far. It would take a while but—"

"No, but he had that box with him full of stuff for his uncle!" I said. "Or I guess he did. How big was it, Larry? It was probably the same one he had behind the ice cream shop the other day."

"I didn't get a good look at it." Larry held out his hands a couple of feet apart. "Maybe this big? This tall?" He changed his hands to show that the box might have been about eighteen inches deep.

"I could bike with an empty box," Terry said. "I think. But if it was full of stuff, probably not. Could you tell if he was carrying it like it was heavy?"

Larry shook his head a little and frowned. "I don't know. Yeah, I guess he held it kind of flat like you would if it had some weight in it. Maybe it had that pack in it that's over in the corner."

"Oh, I forgot about that," Uncle Aaron said. "Do you think we should see what's in the pack? I'm confused. Why would his uncle leave his pack here without getting in the car?"

"Maybe he made that up about his uncle," Terry said. "He told Gary last night that his uncle is gone."

"But the monica! I mean moniker!" Larry said. "The buckle symbol! Old Fish saw it and knew it was his."

"Right." I reached into my pocket again for my notebook. I felt the smooth wooden case, too, but I tried not to think about that. We had enough trouble. "Maybe it's time for that list about what to do next."

"Yeah," Larry said. "So we don't end up like the hobos who starved to death in the warehouse."

"Aw, come on, Larry!" Terry said. "Why do you have to bring that up? I had totally forgotten about that. Why do you read so many books anyway? There are a lot of terrible stories in the world. What's the good of reading them?"

"Look." Uncle Aaron's voice was firm and completely confident. "Everyone calm down. Larry, put that story out of your head now. We are not going to die in here. I feel sure of it. We will get out one way or another."

"You're pretty sure you'll get to say, 'I'm fed up' again sometime?" Larry asked.

"I'm fed up right now," Uncle Aaron said. "With your stories!"

Uncle Aaron could still make jokes, which meant he had things under control. No reason to worry.

Uncle Aaron shone the light on the first list we had made, the list of things we were glad about. It also helped to be reminded of those, especially number three. Uncle Aaron would know what to do. Then I flipped to a blank page. Larry handed me the pen and we composed a list.

1. Search the pack in the corner of the car.
2. Inspect the rest of the car for anything else of interest.
3. Discuss our escape plan if we don't get out soon.

I had suggested that number three read *look for escape possibilities.* But Uncle Aaron had said this sounded too negative. There would be a way to get out. We just had to talk about what that way would be.

"Wow, this car is swaying like crazy!" Larry said. "It feels like we're flying now. I don't know if I'll be able to walk."

"We can walk around the outside wall." Uncle Aaron got to his feet. "At least until we get our—" The train lurched and threw him against the boxcar door. He caught himself with one hand. "As I was saying, just until we get our balance!"

"What's that squeaking noise?" Larry asked. "I bet there's a rat in here."

"You're on a train," Terry said, also getting up. "Why would you be surprised by squeaking noises? There's a thousand hinges and bearings and brakes on this train, and I'm going to take a wild guess and say they squeak sometimes."

"Well, we're about to inspect the car for anything of interest." I looked at the list. "Point number two. If the thing of interest is a rat, we'll deal with it."

"I'm really hoping the thing of interest will be a big cooler full of water and ice." Terry sighed. "It's getting hotter in here by the moment. I bet the floor's not even cool anymore." He bent down and touched the floor and nearly fell over as the train threw us all toward the other side of the car. He did a few acrobatics and caught himself on the other wall without falling. The car was only about ten feet wide, for obvious reasons. It had to fit on the track.

We headed toward the pack, keeping close to the steel walls. I tried not to dwell on the impossibility of cutting our way through those walls.

"Maybe we should have checked the other end first," Larry said as we approached the pack and Terry picked it up. "We already know what's down here. What if we find that Dean's uncle is in here and has been listening to us the whole time?"

A chill shot down my spine. Larry had the worst ideas ever, and the thing I hated most about them was that they were usually plausible. At least theoretical possibilities.

Uncle Aaron, too, was apparently getting tired of his chatter. "You know, Larry," he said, a trace of irritation in his voice, "why don't you focus on not saying the worst possible thing that could happen? Sometimes it helps everyone's morale if we focus on the positives."

"Sorry," Larry said.

"I hate to say it, Uncle Aaron," Terry said as he unzipped the pack. "But every time one of us says that something is the worst thing possible, something even worse happens. We try to avoid naming the worst possible thing."

"We do?" I asked.

"I see," Uncle Aaron said. "Is that why we're here now? Did someone say that the heat was the worst possible thing that could happen today?"

We all laughed a little, which helped everyone relax. Again. We needed laughter in this situation, but it was harder and harder to come by.

Terry frowned as he pulled a blanket out of the pack. "Makes sense to take a blanket along on a train trip, I guess."

"Why are you frowning?" I asked.

"Well, it's a little nicer and softer than I was expecting for a hobo. Although I still think he might have been making the whole thing up. Too bad, I don't think there's any drinks in here. That's what I was hoping for."

"Don't forget, his moniker is on the car," Larry said. He sounded a little subdued after Uncle Aaron's scolding. "Also, if this isn't Buckle's stuff, whose is it?"

At that moment, we all very plainly heard a prolonged squeak at the other end of the car. And we all knew, without discussing it, that the squeak did not come from two pieces of metal rubbing together.

CHAPTER THIRTEEN

Point Number Three

Immediately, we headed toward the noise. Uncle Aaron held the light, and he and Terry led the way, one of them along each wall. I followed Terry, and Larry followed Uncle Aaron.

As we passed the boxcar doors, the beam of flashlight glinted off the wall at the other end of the car. As we grew closer, it shone on something square in one corner.

The cardboard box!

"Did Dean put an animal on this car with us?" Larry asked.

Uncle Aaron and Terry got to the box first. I was closing in on Terry when he jumped like he had touched an electric line. I assumed whatever was in the box had bitten him.

"It's a baby!" he yelled.

"A baby what?" Larry asked, trying to see past Uncle Aaron.

"A baby person!" Terry said. "Duh!"

I burst into uncontrollable laughter. I'm sure it was inappropriate, but Terry saying "Duh" tipped me over the edge. He said it as if it were perfectly natural to find a baby human in a corner of a moving box car somewhere between Elkhart and the western plains.

Whether it was my laughter or not I don't know, but the baby began to wail like its heart was broken.

"Gary, maybe you should be quiet," Uncle Aaron said, with a little more irritation in his voice than when he had reproved Larry.

I bit down hard on my lower lip to stifle my laughter and squeezed in beside Terry to have a look.

In the bottom of the cardboard box, wrapped in a thin blanket, a baby wailed. It was crying so hard its small fists shook, unless that was from the shaking of the train. The four of us stood above the box, staring down in shock and disbelief. One look at the baby had removed the laughter from me, but I found that I was still biting down on my lip. The pain felt appropriate somehow.

"What is going on?" Uncle Aaron finally said. He had to raise his voice to be heard above the train and the screaming baby. "What has Dean gotten us into? Larry, do you think this is the box that Dean was carrying?"

"Yes, I think so."

"I think it's the one I saw him with," I said. "But it was definitely empty then. Hey! Could this be the child Dean's mom was yelling about? The one she couldn't help care for?"

"I don't know," Uncle Aaron said. "But this is turning into

a much more serious situation than just the four of us trying to get out of a boxcar."

We didn't need Uncle Aaron to tell us that.

"Could Dean be trying to set us up and make us look like we kidnapped this baby?" Larry asked.

"Yes, he could be." Uncle Aaron's voice was tight. "But there's nothing we can do about protecting our reputation or proving our innocence now. What we need to do now is figure out how to provide for this baby."

"Well, here's where having Larry along will stand us in good stead." Terry turned to our encyclopedia brother, talking loudly. "I'm sorry for what I said about you reading too much. What can you tell us about the care of babies?"

Larry's face looked as empty as a house after the moving van pulls away. "I don't think I've ever read one word about taking care of babies!"

"Aw, come on!" Terry spread his hands out like he couldn't believe it as the car careened to the right. He fell against the wall, and the rest of us caught ourselves on it too. The baby quieted for two seconds, then resumed screaming. "Seriously, Larry!" Terry shouted. "You've read the handbook for all this ridiculous stuff like how to milk a camel in a sandstorm and why it's important to freeze dry polar bear livers if you're at the North Pole." Like I said, Terry can develop into quite a wordsmith when he gets mad. "How could you not have read the handbook on how to take care of a baby?"

"I never read anything about milking a camel in a sandstorm!"

Larry yelled back. "Or about—"

"Stop, everyone," Uncle Aaron said. We all fell silent, except the baby. "I think we should pick the baby out of the box, maybe, and see if there are any obvious problems with it." It sounded a little like he was talking about a watermelon or something, but I certainly wasn't going to point this out. "Then, we're going to have a prayer meeting. I don't know why I didn't suggest it before."

Uncle Aaron handed Larry the flashlight and got down on his knees beside the box. He reached into it carefully and put one hand around each side of the baby's stomach and lifted. The baby's head sagged back into the box, as if it didn't want to come along. The baby howled louder than before.

"You know," I yelled, "I think I vaguely remember Mom telling me that you have to support the head on a baby!"

"Good point," Uncle Aaron said. He shifted tactics and slid his left hand behind the baby's head. This worked. Not only did the baby emerge from the box in one geometric plane, but he or she quit crying. He still treated the baby somewhat like a watermelon, holding it out in front of him. He looked remarkably pleased that the baby had quieted down.

"No need to read the handbook about babies," he said. "Gary can write it!"

"No!" I said. "I don't think there are handbooks. I think it's natural human instinct to know how to take care of them."

"If it is natural human instinct," Uncle Aaron said, "then it either doesn't hit until after you have a child, or I'm not human."

"He's sizing you up!" Terry said.

It did appear that way. The baby's eyes dialed in on Uncle Aaron. Then its mouth turned into an O as if Uncle Aaron was the most astonishing occurrence on the face of the known world.

We all laughed, and once again, it released some of the tension.

"Okay, Gary," Larry said, "why don't you keep on with your vague memories of what Mom told you about babies. What are the most essential needs?"

"Probably water," Terry said dismally. "Of which, if you forget, we have none."

I hadn't forgotten. My mouth felt like paper.

"Diapers?" I suggested. "Blankets? Oh! That blanket in the pack is for him, I bet!"

Somehow, we were gradually assigning the pronoun *he* to the nameless baby.

"Right!" Terry had brought it with him when we came to investigate the squeak, and he now picked it off the floor. "Maybe there's a bottle or something in here too."

Terry turned the bag inside out. It was a small canvas bag with a strap for wearing over the shoulder. The blanket fell to the boxcar floor, along with a flurry of diapers. No bottle.

"Well, at least he's happy right now." Uncle Aaron shifted and slid to a sitting position. I sat beside him. When he rested the baby on his leg, it began to wail again.

"Nope, wrong way." Uncle Aaron moved him back into the handhold position, and he quieted down.

"What's that?" Larry pointed to the diapers.

Terry kicked at them. "Diapers?"

"No, I thought I saw a note in there." He bent down and lifted the diapers one by one. Sure enough, on the floor of the boxcar, he found a piece of lined paper. He picked it up and held it close to the light. I jumped up to look at it too and saw that a few sentences had been scrawled on the page. Larry read them aloud.

"Buckle, you are family. Do something for this-" Larry paused, frowning at the scribbled word. "-child. Our sister is headed for the jug, and I can't take care of her with my own man in there. Take to a mission or church if you have to. Maybe better out of in. Thanks, Liz."

"Oh!" Uncle Aaron said. "Buckle was supposed to get this baby. Is that what this note is saying?"

"What's the jug?" Terry asked.

"Jail, I think," Larry said. "I read that in my hobo book."

I studied the note. "If this person says *our sister*, then Buckle must be her brother. You think Dean's mom wrote this note?"

"Right!" I sat down beside Uncle Aaron again. The pieces were falling together. Some of the pieces, at least. "She sent Dean to give this baby to Buckle, but instead they all abandoned the baby and left him with us."

"Right again," Larry sighed. "But why would the mother not want her own child?"

"Because she's going to jail." I stared at Larry. "You said that is what jug means. She won't be able to take care of him in jail anyway."

"Probably so." Uncle Aaron frowned. The baby stayed quiet,

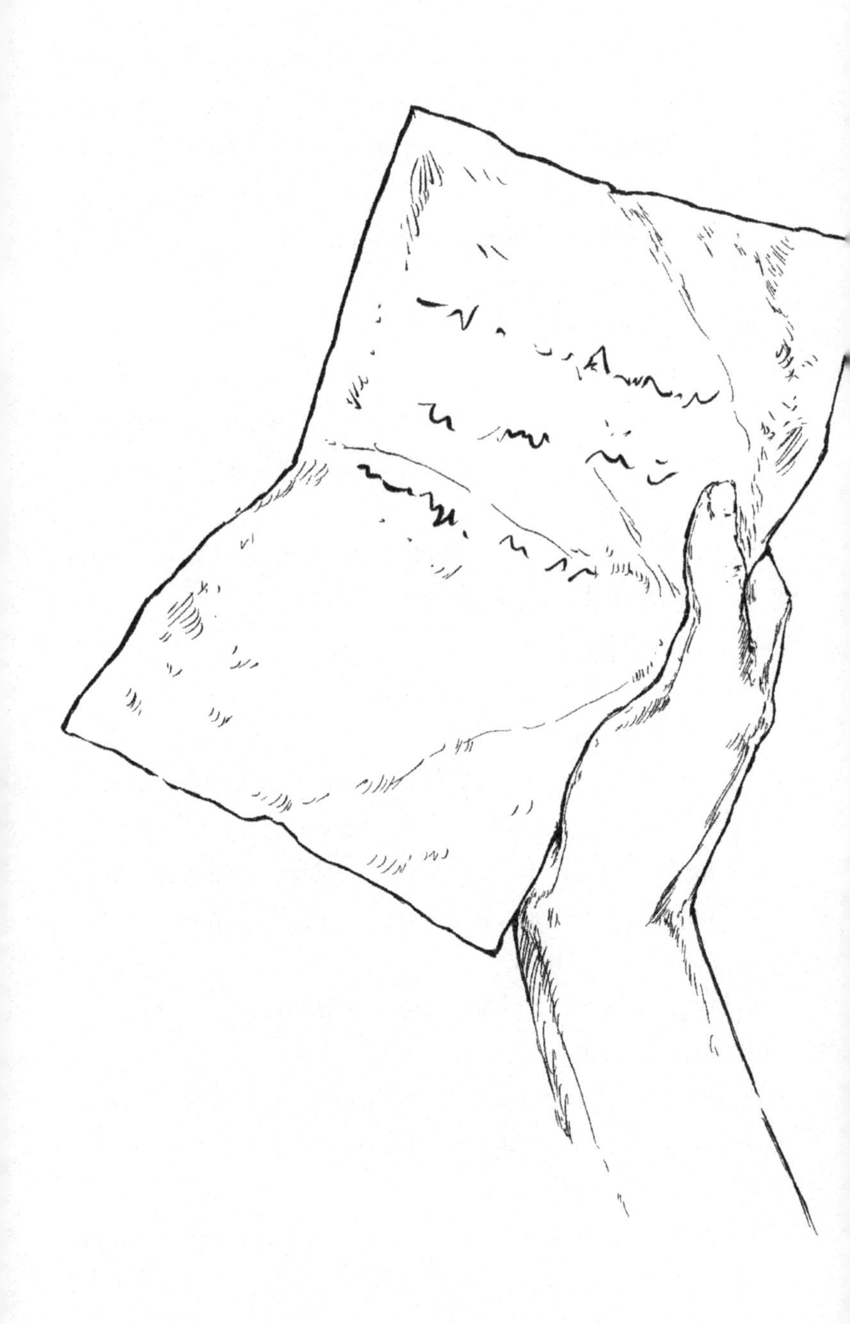

still staring at Uncle Aaron. "What was that line about *out of in*? What sense does that make? Can I see it?"

Larry squatted on the other side of Uncle Aaron and showed him the paper.

"Oh, the *IN* is capitalized," Uncle Aaron said. "She wanted Buckle to smuggle this baby out of Indiana on the freight train. But I guess he figured out that might be illegal and got cold feet."

"Do you think Dean knew that Buckle abandoned the baby and decided he'd better send us with the baby?" I asked. "To take care of it?"

No one answered.

The baby started to cry. Again.

I looked at Uncle Aaron. "What should we do?"

"Get out your list of blessings," Uncle Aaron called back over the baby's screams, "and cross out number three."

CHAPTER FOURTEEN

Unexpected Situations

I slowly turned to my list of blessings after Uncle Aaron told me to cross out number three. I knew generally what number three said, but I wanted to see it again.

> 3. Uncle Aaron knows what to do no matter what happens.

As the baby wailed and the train rocked back and forth, I leaned against the wall of the boxcar, sick at heart. Finding a crying baby in the boxcar was way worse than finding a hobo. How had we not searched the car right away? And why had we not heard the baby before? We had passed off the little squeaks as something that was part of the train.

If the baby died on our hands, would we all go to prison as

murderers?

Honestly, though, I think I was in despair because Uncle Aaron seemed to be discouraged. If he had stayed positive, I could have hung on to hope too.

At least Uncle Aaron remembered the prayer meeting idea. We huddled together and prayed the loudest prayers we had ever prayed in our lives, competing with the rocking train and the wailing of the baby. We even asked God to calm the baby and help us figure out what to do with him.

Our prayer ended. The baby cried on.

"Uncle Aaron!" Larry said.

"Yeah?"

"You know you were talking earlier about people who tell God they'll serve Him and then He gives them a different assignment than they expected."

"A different what?"

"Assignment!" Larry yelled.

"Oh, right!"

I expected Larry to go on. He didn't, and he was still holding the flashlight so I couldn't see his face. Suddenly I thought of something.

"Larry! We've got to turn the flashlight off and use it only when we need it! What if the batteries die?"

"You're right!" Larry flicked off the light.

"Wait." Uncle Aaron was jiggling the baby up and down, which seemed to help, but it still cried on and off. "Let's do one more thing with that light. Check in the box. There was a blanket kind of thing in the bottom and maybe there is something else down there."

"Why didn't we think of that?" I asked. The three of us dove for the box and ripped out the blanket. Several items shook loose and fell into the box. Larry picked up a plastic container labeled *Formula*.

"The formula for what?" Larry asked. "Some kind of mathematical equation we're supposed to do?"

"That's baby food!" Uncle Aaron said. "Now, that's one thing I do know!"

"Here's a bottle!" Terry yelled.

"Here's a thermos of water!" I hollered.

Giddy with relief, we took our loot over to Uncle Aaron.

"Is the water for us?" Terry asked.

"No," Uncle Aaron said. "The formula is probably a powder, and you mix it with water to make milk."

"Oh." Terry swallowed. So did I. The closeness of the water was painful. But we should save it for the baby, who surely would be the first to die of the five of us if it got nothing.

"Okay." Larry had taken the lid off the plastic container. Sure enough, there was powder inside, along with a small plastic scoop. I unscrewed the lid of the bottle.

"There's some water in here already," I said. "But how much powder do we mix in?"

We all looked at the bottle. It seemed like the answer to that question was crucial. It might save the baby's life if we got it right. But if we messed it up, and wasted some of the water, the baby, and maybe all of us, could die of thirst.

"What's that on the scoop?" Uncle Aaron asked.

Larry held the small scoop directly under the beam of the flashlight and read aloud. "One scoop for two ounces."

"Ounces?" Terry sounded totally discouraged. "How are we supposed to know how much an ounce of water is?"

"Maybe the bottle is marked," Uncle Aaron said.

"Surely not," Terry said. "Are babies that scientific?"

I held up the bottle, and sure enough, there was a ruler on the side of it with numbers from 1-4. The bottle had four ounces of water already in it.

I held the bottle while Larry carefully measured out the powder.

"Put the lid on and shake it," Uncle Aaron suggested.

"Wow!" Terry said. "You need to write the handbook, Uncle Aaron."

We got the bottle into the baby's mouth and things instantly changed for the better. The baby sucked furiously as if it was starving, and totally quit crying. We all sighed and relaxed a little. Terry fell back on the boxcar floor.

"This is our chance to talk!" Larry turned off the light. "Assuming he'll start in yelling again when the bottle is empty."

"He was probably crying because he was hungry," Uncle Aaron said.

"Babies cry when they're hungry?" Terry's voice, coming from the floor, sounded far away in the darkness.

"Of course!" I said. "You basically cry when you're hungry!"

"No, I don't, or I'd be crying right now!"

Uncle Aaron broke into a hearty laugh, as if he had just swallowed the final bite of a big meal. The truth was, we were all hungry. But we felt much better now that we had solved the problem of the screaming baby.

"Hey, boys, I need to apologize." Uncle Aaron's voice grew serious after his laugh. "Larry reminded me of what I said earlier and he's absolutely right. For some reason God allowed us to end up here with this baby. Who knows, maybe we'll be falsely accused, but maybe we will be the means of saving the baby's life. Wouldn't that be great?"

We were quiet for a moment, then Terry's faraway voice came again. "I'm so mad at Dean! I think I'm madder at him than I was last week when I first met him! How could he do this to us after we took him out for pizza and befriended him?"

The train went over a mighty bump that nearly shook our joints apart, as if it was angry too.

"What was the definition of long-suffering?" Larry asked. "Something about ongoing offenses."

"Lasting offense," I said.

"Yes, that's it. Maybe that's Dean. A lasting offense."

"You can say that again," Terry mumbled.

Uncle Aaron, however, had not exhausted his words of wisdom. "I'm not convinced that Dean is totally in the wrong here."

I heard rustling in Terry's corner and his voice came from higher up, so I knew he had sat up. "How could he not be?"

I was so glad Uncle Aaron was back to his old self that I felt almost hopeful about our situation.

"Well...the wheels are still turning in my brain. Let's turn on the light, Larry, and Gary you write a few things down that we know so far. First, Dean almost certainly had just put the baby in the boxcar, so he knew he was in here. Second, if someone gave him this baby to give to Buckle, that person must have trusted him with the baby. Third, if Dean saw that Buckle was not going to show up, he had to find someone to look out for the baby while it gets out of Indiana."

"Or go with the baby himself," Terry said. "Why not do that?"

"What if he knew he couldn't manage it himself?" Uncle Aaron said.

"Well, we don't know if we can manage this!" Terry was still seething.

I scrawled down the facts as they talked.

1. Dean knew about the baby.
2. Someone trusted Dean with the baby.
3. Buckle didn't show up.
4. The baby needed someone to watch it.
5. Possibly Dean didn't think he could.

"I get it, Terry." Uncle Aaron's voice was kind. "But I suspect that Dean was put in a bad position too. What if his mom said he had to take the baby to Buckle and dare not bring it back? What was he going to do, without abandoning the baby in the boxcar and letting it die?"

Between the noises of the train, we could hear the baby still chowing down his lunch. I felt sick thinking of what would have happened if the baby were still lying in the box, alone, screaming. Uncle Aaron had a point.

"So, you think he saw us and thought, *Hey, I wonder if I can trap them in the boxcar with the baby so it has someone to care for it?*" Terry asked.

"Possibly," Uncle Aaron said.

"He even put the pack on the opposite side of the car from the baby." I scribbled a quick sketch of a boxcar as I talked. "So that we wouldn't see the baby right away."

"How old is that baby, anyway?" Terry asked. I could tell that Uncle Aaron's calmness had calmed him. "Is there any way to tell?"

"Hmmm," Larry said. "Too bad you can't check its teeth like they do for horses. Do you think he's a year old?"

"I was thinking more like three days old," Uncle Aaron said. "He's pretty small. I don't know the numbers, but I'm thinking that by the time a baby is a year old they can sit up in a high chair and smash their birthday cake. Pretty sure I remember you doing that, Larry."

"You *do* know lots of things about babies!" I said.

"Watching a baby sitting in a high chair is totally different from being responsible for keeping it alive," Uncle Aaron said. "For instance, I have no idea how often a baby needs to have its diaper changed."

At the mention of this topic, we all froze. It seemed very

unlikely that a baby would survive having its diaper changed by us, in a moving boxcar.

"Well," Larry finally ventured. "If there are handbooks on babies, the diaper-changing instructions would have to include a caution clause."

"Like what?" Terry asked.

"Something like, 'If no diaper-changing experts are available, change the diaper every other day instead of every day.'"

Uncle Aaron laughed. "I'm pretty sure my sisters talked about having to change diapers more than every day."

"They knew how to do it!" Larry said. "They weren't endangering the life of the baby by doing it."

Clearly, Larry and I were on the same wavelength about this.

"Well, I have a suggestion," Uncle Aaron said. "How about we hold off on the diaper business at least until we come to a stop."

"What are we going to do if the train stops?" I asked. "We should probably have a plan."

"How about we draw straws," Uncle Aaron said. "Two of us will change the baby's diaper in case we don't get help at that stop. The other two of us will pound like crazy on the doors of the car and yell for help."

CHAPTER FIFTEEN

Drawing Straws

Of course, we all wanted to get the pounding job instead of the diaper-changing job. Terry tried to argue that he would be better at pounding than anyone else and should be excused from the possibility of having to change the diaper.

I called him out. "Last night you were talking about how easy it would be to change diapers instead of pull weeds!"

Uncle Aaron waved him off too.

"I'm pretty sure we'll all be good at whatever God calls us to do," he said. "Gary, tear four pieces of paper, two long and two short. Mix them up in your hand, and then let us pick them in the dark. Whoever gets the long ones will pound. The ones with the short ones will change the diaper."

With Larry holding the light, I opened my notebook and tore off three strips. The one strip I tore in half, making two. Then I held them in my hand so I couldn't see anything but the tops. Larry switched off the light and selected a strip. I then reached out my hand to Uncle Aaron and Terry who each selected one too. That left me with the last one.

"The moment of truth!" Larry cried, turning on the flashlight.

We held up our strips. Larry and Uncle Aaron had the short ones. Terry and I had the long ones.

"Well, Larry," Uncle Aaron said. "You and I got the hardest job, but we'll figure it out!"

I stared at the long strip in my hand. "You know, Uncle Aaron, I don't know how to change a diaper. But now that I think about it, I kind of got my fill of pounding and yelling the other week in the tunnel. Besides, you're taller and might get more attention. Want to trade?"

"Think you two can handle the baby?"

In the flashlight's beam, I could see that the baby had finished the bottle. But he had not resumed crying. He was sticking his little fists into the air and waving them around as if delivering a speech that was crucial to the survival of humanity. Or at least the survival of the five of us in the boxcar. He looked downright cute.

"Sure!" I said. "Hand him over."

This request felt like a reckless act of daring similar to jumping into the Niagara River a hundred yards above the falls. But we were living in perilous times and normal rules did not count.

Uncle Aaron handed the baby to me. I almost panicked as his body kind of settled, like a bag of wheat or something. It didn't seem to hold its own weight like a cat or a dog. His head rolled a little. But nothing bad happened after he settled, and I managed to balance my arm just right so his head quit rolling to the side. The baby kept on waving its fists, taking the world to task.

"I think he's full of ideas about how to get out of this boxcar," I said. "Too bad he can't talk yet."

"Speaking of that." Uncle Aaron stretched and got to his feet, touching the side of the car for support. "Terry, let's walk around this car and pick our best spot for pounding."

"On the doors, right?" Terry jumped up too.

"Yes, probably. Let's look for something to pound with."

Larry went with them, holding the light. It was crazy to watch them walk, as the train jolted them and their beam of light, first right and then left, forward and back. I saw Uncle Aaron and Terry beating on the side of the train with their fists for practice, creating fast-moving dancing shadows on the wall. I was glad I had traded. They had trouble walking on two good legs.

After their circuit, they returned and sat beside me and the baby again.

"Not one thing on this train to use as a hammer," Terry said. "I guess we'll be pounding with our fists."

"There's the flashlight," I said. "It might not survive though."

Larry's flashlight was pretty heavy duty, but it was made of plastic. No one wanted to risk losing the light. After they were all seated, Larry turned it off to save battery.

We sat in silence for a bit. I finally spoke.

"Well, if I wouldn't be searching for Dr. Jefferson like this, life would be so much easier right now."

"That's not true," Larry said. "We came here more for Dean's sake than anything. Crumb Boss already told us that Buckle probably doesn't know anything more about Dr. Jefferson than he does."

"Yes, but we wouldn't have even come to the Hobo Jungle if we wouldn't be looking for Dr. Jefferson."

"I'm not sad we went to the Hobo Jungle," Terry said. "That was interesting. I suppose if we end up starving to death, I might be sad, but..."

"We aren't going to starve to death." Uncle Aaron's voice sounded sure, and we all breathed a sigh of relief. Even if Larry's story of boxcars abandoned in warehouses still circled through my mind, I trusted Uncle Aaron's intuition.

"Gary, do you think the international fugitive got your letter yet?" Larry asked.

I thought back to last week at the library. I had written a letter to the international fugitive, who had been arrested for stealing rare artifacts from museums. I had written to ask him about his friend Bruce who left town on the CHEL. We hadn't known at the time that those letters stood for the train that went from Chicago to Elkhart.

"We don't really need him anyway," I said. "Dean already told us what the letters mean."

"Yes, but you never know what else the international fugitive might know."

"Like all the crimes Dr. Jefferson has committed? How many

people's legs he cut off when they didn't need to be cut off?"

"No, of course not!" Larry sounded irritated. "I mean more clues to finding him or finding out more about him. Why do you always assume the worst about him?"

I didn't answer. I figured Uncle Aaron was about to reprimand me for my comment, and I didn't want to make it worse or sound like a whiner.

Uncle Aaron did speak next, but he was talking to Larry.

"Give him some space to talk it out, Larry. I don't think it's likely that Dr. Jefferson cut off people's legs for no reason. But if someone cut off my leg and then disappeared, I would have to work through some struggles too, I think."

I was glad it was dark because I felt tears forming. I suppose crying was as dumb as my outburst of laughter had been when Terry said "Duh!" about the baby. But Uncle Aaron sticking up for me actually made me much less worried about Dr. Jefferson. With an uncle like that, who cared about what a surgeon had done six years before?

"How far do you think this train will go before it stops?" Terry's question came from down low again, so he must have sprawled out on the floor like normal.

"Probably Chicago," Uncle Aaron said. "Unless there's a stop part way. I looked at my watch when we had the light on, and it's been about an hour and a half since we left. I'm guessing we are going directly to Chicago, or we would have stopped already."

"If only there were one little hole to look out of so we would know where we are," Larry said.

"Or, so we could catch rain water." Terry's voice sounded gloomy. "All I can think about is water. I see it in the dark. Water on pipes in the basement. A bathtub full of water. Ice cubes floating."

"Lemonade." Larry chimed in. "Watermelon chunks."

"Hey, it was my list," Terry protested.

"It can be everyone's list," Larry said. "It might even make us less thirsty. If only it wouldn't be so hot. Cold water sounds good, with ice cubes floating and all, but I could even use warm water."

"Root beer," Uncle Aaron said. "Wouldn't a can of that taste good right now? What do you all want for your first drink when we get out of here? If you could have anything you want?"

"I want a big jug of plain old water," Terry said.

"I'm sticking with lemonade." Larry smacked his lips as if he was drinking it right then and there.

"I'd like some of that grape drink Larry makes for us." I could almost feel the edge of the glass on my lips, ice clinking against the sides. "What's your pick, Baby?"

"He's the only one that doesn't need anything," Terry said. "He already had a big drink. If we only knew we were going to get out, we could divide his water among us."

No one said anything for a minute.

"I think we're going to get out," Uncle Aaron said. "But I don't know how soon. And my feeling is that we should try to keep the water for the baby as long as possible."

Fear gripped my heart again. Yes, Uncle Aaron felt good about our prospects. But not so good that he wanted to divide the water. We might be in this car for days. Would we survive?

"I think I'll take a nap," Terry said. "What else is there to do?"

The boxcar grew quiet as we rested and dozed. I was in a dreamy half-wake state when I heard Larry's voice.

"Hey! Doesn't it seem like the train is slowing?"

We all paid attention to the sounds of the train and the feel of the vibrations.

"You're right!" Uncle Aaron said. "It could be slowing for a turn or something."

We listened for another ten seconds, and then Terry bounced to his feet. "Where's the flashlight, Larry? Turn it on! It's stopping!"

CHAPTER SIXTEEN

Riding the Rails

Uncle Aaron leaped to his feet too. The train really was stopping. Larry snapped on the light and swung it back and forth between the two boxcar doors. Terry took the side farthest from me, and Uncle Aaron took the door a few feet from where we sat.

"Let's start!" Uncle Aaron hollered. "Someone might hear us as we come in!"

Terry and Uncle Aaron beat on the boxcar doors like they were trying to catch the attention of a deaf man. The baby jerked and began to wail.

"Let the baby cry!" Uncle Aaron said. "He might get someone's attention!"

The pounding was so loud I couldn't imagine how we could be missed.

"We're going to wear out our fists soon!" Uncle Aaron shouted to Terry. He reached down and snatched off one of his shoes. "I'm going to try some of this too!"

In the dim light, I saw Uncle Aaron gripping the toe of his tennis shoe and bringing it down hard on the boxcar door. It made a tremendous slapping sound against the metal.

Terry followed suit, just as the train jolted and stopped.

"The shoe doesn't work as well for rattling the door," Uncle Aaron said. "But we can use it to give our fists a break. You use the shoe while I pound and then we'll switch."

Any minute now, we would hear the latch being lifted on the outside of the boxcar door. I was sure of it. The racket that Uncle Aaron and Terry were making sounded like something that would be heard across Chicago.

"Gary! Listen to me!" Larry was shouting. Apparently, he had been trying to get my attention and I had not noticed. "What about changing the diaper?"

"Oh, right."

The baby continued to cry.

"Are you sure we should try if he's already crying?"

Larry looked grimly at me. "I don't know! How are we supposed to know?"

"We're surely about to be rescued! We can turn him over to the police and they can do it."

"You think police know how to change diapers?" Larry looked doubtful.

"There's got to be a class for that somewhere in their training!

I'm afraid we'll really mess it up if we try now when he's crying."

"Keep going, Terry!" Uncle Aaron encouraged. "You know how big these train yards are. And if there are other trains coming and going, there may be only a short amount of time for someone to hear us."

"I have an idea, Larry. Get a diaper and see if you can figure out how the thing works."

Larry nodded and swung the light across the boxcar floor until he found the pack that contained the diapers. He pulled one out and unfolded it in the beam of light.

"What are these?" Larry pulled at something that looked like tabs of tape.

"Maybe to keep them on?"

"Yeah maybe. But how do we know which is the front and which is the back?"

This seemed to be an insurmountable question. Larry flipped the diaper around a few times, then looked at me with a blank face. "No idea."

"Well, I think we're failing the test," I said. "We should have consulted with Uncle Aaron and Terry before the train stopped."

Shortly after I said the *train stopped*, the boxcar jerked and pulled forward.

"Oh, no," we all groaned.

"Keep going," Uncle Aaron shouted. "This might be the moment we go past someone who hears us. Help! Is anyone out there?"

The baby cried, Uncle Aaron and Terry pounded, and the

train picked up speed. Faster and faster and faster. *Ka. Thud. Ka-thud. Ka-thud, ka-thud, ka-thud.* All hope was gone. Uncle Aaron's arm fell to his side. Terry quit too, and they both came back to join us.

With the pounding silenced, the baby quieted down.

"If that was Chicago..." Larry snapped off the flashlight. His voice sounded hopeless. "If that was Chicago, then we're headed for the Great Plains. Maybe to the Pacific Ocean. It will take days to get there."

I had always wanted to go see the West. We had borrowed books from the library with photos of the Grand Canyon and Mount Rushmore and redwood trees so tall you could cut a tunnel in the base of the trunk for cars to drive through.

But going west in an enclosed boxcar with a crying baby, one container of water, and no food? This was a different matter.

"I read in a survival book that people can live for three days without water," Larry added.

"We have a little water," Terry said. "Surely the baby can share a few drops with us. My tongue is already sticking to the inside of my mouth."

"So maybe if we have a teaspoon of water here and there we can survive for four days." As I said this, I wondered if there was a mathematical equation to figure out how long humans can live with small amounts of water? A graph of some sort, maybe. With one teaspoon a day, a person could survive for four days. Two teaspoons a day might increase a person's life span to five days.

But then, a baby was so small it would need a different graph.

And how would we know the correct measurements so everyone would have a chance to survive?

What if no one ever checked this boxcar and we just...? But then, it wouldn't matter anymore. But it would matter to our parents, who would have no idea what had happened to us. Surely Dean would confess if he heard we were missing.

"Dean knows we're here," I said. "If he hears we're missing, surely he'll tell someone."

"He hates us." Terry sounded certain. "Why else would he do this to us?"

"Let's say he hates us," Larry said. "But does he hate the baby? Why did he put us in here if not to watch the baby? Surely he'll at least notify someone to tell them where the baby is."

I was still holding the baby, and although I couldn't see him, I wondered if he had fallen asleep because there sure wasn't much motion from him.

"Wouldn't count on it," Terry mumbled.

"You know, I don't think that was Chicago." Uncle Aaron's voice broke through the gloomy conversation. "First I thought it was. But I think we would have stopped longer than that in Chicago. It also doesn't seem like enough time has passed to get us into Chicago."

"Really?" I had imagined us halfway to Iowa already. Could we still be in Indiana? A flicker of hope brightened my inner being.

"Maybe it was a quick stop in Chicago," Larry said.

"Maybe." Uncle Aaron's voice still sounded hopeful. "But I'm guessing we will be pulling into another stop before long."

"It's too bad we don't have anything to do to pass the time," Larry sighed. "We can't play the ABC game like we do on road trips."

"What's the ABC game?" Uncle Aaron asked.

"It's not a game," Terry said. "It's work."

"No, it's not!" Larry almost certainly rolled his eyes in the dark, but I couldn't see him. "You look for all the letters of the alphabet outside of the vehicle. Like on license plates or billboards or buildings. Whoever gets to Z first wins."

"What if I find a Z right away?" Uncle Aaron asked. "Does that count?"

"No, of course not," Larry said. "You have to find them in the right order. Haven't you ever played it before? I thought Mom said she played it on road trips in her childhood."

"By the time he was born, Grandpa and Grandma didn't force their children to play alphabet games," Terry said.

"Hey!" Larry's voice sounded excited. "Gary! Hey! I just thought about something! Crumb Boss said he was going to take the wooden box and the locket to the post office today. He must have an address for Dr. Jefferson!"

"You're right. How did I miss that?" I would have jumped up, but thankfully I caught myself before dumping the baby on the floor.

"How did we all miss that?" Uncle Aaron said. "Larry, you get the delayed reaction award today! But you know, we were all pretty nervous about being accused of stealing the locket ourselves, and I guess that post office comment flew over our heads."

"First thing we do when we get out of here alive," Terry said. "Hunt down Crumb Boss for the address."

I didn't like Terry's wording. *Get out of here alive.* Somehow it sounded more like a reminder that we might *not* get out of here alive. But I agreed with him otherwise.

"Hey." I stiffened, and the baby squirmed. "Is the train slowing down?"

"The heat is playing tricks with your mind," Terry said.

"No, I think you're right!" Uncle Aaron leaped up. "It is! Terry, to your post! Give us some light, Larry!"

Terry leaped to his feet as Larry snapped on the light, and his exaggerated shadow sprang up the wall of the boxcar like a frightened monster. Uncle Aaron had his hand against the boxcar wall and was feeling his way toward the door. With Larry's light, he was there with one stride.

"Don't get your hopes up too high!" I yelled to the others. "The train might stop at a bunch of little stations before it gets to Chicago!"

"Doesn't mean that someone can't rescue us at a little station!" Uncle Aaron yelled back. He was his positive self again, and it was infecting me with hope.

The train chugged along slowly for what seemed like half an hour, but probably wasn't. The baby remained quiet.

Finally, the boxcar eased to a stop. Terry and Uncle Aaron began yelling and pounding again, and the baby jerked and began to scream.

The fear returned. We had thought it would work last time,

but no one had come. What if the same thing happened again, and this time it was Chicago and the next stop was Denver? Or San Francisco?

Suddenly, I heard the screech of metal from under Uncle Aaron's pounding fists. The door he was pounding on rolled back and we found ourselves flooded with bright afternoon light.

CHAPTER SEVENTEEN

South Chicago

The shock of freedom and light was almost too great a change to absorb. Terry kept pounding on his door for a few seconds until he realized that the light was from an open door and we no longer needed to pound. Once he quit making the racket, the baby quit crying. I was still blinking my eyes and adjusting them to the brightness. It was as if we were standing next to the sun. But in a few moments, I found that I could keep my eyes open long enough to take in my surroundings.

Larry had moved toward the open door, holding the flashlight which was still turned on. Terry had turned and was standing behind Uncle Aaron. Uncle Aaron looked down at a man standing beside the train, his head and shoulders above the level of the boxcar floor.

The man had an unruly, red-tinged beard and mustache and

a bald head. A long wooden pipe stuck from his lips, similar to the pipe Old Fish had. The man's face was red and kind of puffy, although I suspected the red color was from the heat. He wore a limp gray T-shirt and did not look at all like a railroad security officer.

He removed his pipe from his mouth, so it could fall open in amazement. It was pretty clear that he wasn't expecting to find a grown man and three boys staring at him. And he probably hadn't even seen the baby yet. He blinked rapidly, as if he was the one who had been in the darkness and suddenly pushed into the bright sunlight.

Uncle Aaron leaped to the ground, and I knew what he was thinking. All three of us moved to the edge of the car. We were not going to be trapped again.

The man on the ground took a step back into the middle of the empty track between our train and the next train. "Wasn't expecting to see a crowd here. Just looking for a..." he trailed off and stuck his head into the car, squinting. "Ah, there she is! I was looking for that baby."

"You? Were looking? For the baby?" Uncle Aaron stared at the man, then back at the baby, still in my arms.

"Yeah." The man was about twice the size of Uncle Aaron. Not gigantic like the security guard at the rail yard, but round. "But I didn't hear she was coming with an escort."

"We didn't know she was either," Uncle Aaron said.

"She!" Larry hissed to me. "It's a *she*!"

"I heard! Get the box so we can put her back in."

"Well then how...?" Red Beard shook his head and stared at us as if he had been struck dumb.

I carefully laid the baby in the box, and the three of us sat on the edge of the car, listening.

"That's exactly what we were wondering." Uncle Aaron looked up at us.

"Oh." Larry looked down at the man who continued blinking in the sunlight. "You're Buckle, aren't you? Are you Dean's uncle?"

"Yup." Red Beard stuck out a hand to Uncle Aaron. "Name's Buckle. That's my niece you've got."

Uncle Aaron's eyes widened, and his mouth opened like he was about to say something.

Terry beat him. "Wait. We thought you were in Elkhart. They said you were there last night and that you were supposed to take care of the baby."

"Yup. What do you mean, s'posed to? I'm here, aren't I? Don't know nothing about taking care of no baby, but I'm here all the same."

Uncle Aaron shook his head in confusion. He reached for the box with the baby in it. "You boys hop down before this train tries to leave again."

Seconds before, we had been afraid we would die of thirst. Now it appeared that we had a good chance of being alive next week.

But would we be accused of kidnapping a baby?

"Get the baby's stuff!" I said.

Terry walked back to retrieve the baby's pack, then leaped off

the car in one smooth motion, landing on a wooden tie. Larry and I slid over the side onto the crushed rock.

The baby began to wail again, and I felt sick at heart for its future. I was completely confused by what was going on, but it sounded like Buckle would take the baby. And if he didn't know how to care for her, who would?

"Why didn't you pick up the baby when you were in Elkhart?" Larry asked. "We saw your moniker on the train." He turned and pointed to the buckle, which was still there of course, date and all.

"I didn't hear about the baby needing a place to stay until after I got back home to Chicago this morning early." Buckle smiled a knowing smile, as if he was pleased to know a little more about life than these sad boys who had been locked in a boxcar. "Dean drew that on there for me and told me what time the train was coming and what kind of cars were on either side of this car. Didn't really need that though, with all that pounding and racket ya'll made and the baby crying."

"Dean drew your symbol?" Larry and Terry and I all said some version of this question at the same time. I felt like every time I made an assumption about Dean I found it was wrong.

"Sure! I've taught him my signature. He can do it as well as me."

"So why did he lock us in with the baby?" Larry asked.

Uncle Aaron was trying to rock the baby's box to make her happy, but it wasn't really working. "Do you want to take her?" He motioned to me to hold the box. Then, after picking the baby out, he held her out to Buckle.

Buckle held up his hands in front of him as if in defense. "I don't know nothing about caring for no baby! I'm here to pick her up and deliver her to my wife to see if she knows what to do. And I don't have any idea how ya'll got locked in with her. Maybe Dean wanted someone to look out for her. She's a bit small for rail riding in my opinion, but my sister said there was no choice but to get her out of the state."

"Where are we anyway?" Larry asked. "Chicago?"

We couldn't see anything because we were standing between two trains.

"Yup. South Chicago, not the main yard uptown. This is a smaller one at least, easier to find trains. Is that her luggage?" Buckle nodded toward the box and pack.

"Yes." I looked into the box and saw a small plastic thing that looked like it was meant for the baby to suck on. I was pretty sure I had seen babies with them before, although I couldn't remember what they were called. I pulled it out and put it in her mouth and she calmed down dramatically.

"Looks like you all know how to take care of her," Buckle sighed. "You even have her pacifier. I don't know what we're going to do with her. Haven't even told my wife about her yet."

I opened my mouth to explain that I hadn't even remembered the name of the plastic thing until he said *pacifier.* But Uncle Aaron started talking, eyebrows raised.

"You haven't told your wife that you're bringing home a baby?"

"I hear you, man, I hear you." Buckle had been holding his

pipe ever since taking it out, but he now put it back in his mouth, as if he, like the baby, needed comfort. "I'm not looking forward to it, but what is a person supposed to do when family needs help? My sister got arrested yesterday at work. I guess she knew it might happen, so she tried to get our other sister—that's Dean's mom—to take the baby but she refused. So it's up to me to figure it out I guess."

"Wait—at work? Was it at Rocky's restaurant?"

"Don't know the name, but it was a little restaurant in Stratford."

Did that mean our waitress was Dean's aunt?

I wanted to ask why the sister was going to jail, but I decided it probably wasn't in good taste. However, we had other things to worry about. As he talked on, Buckle answered my question without being asked.

"Been telling those girls to leave the drugs alone, but they won't listen. We was all raised in a traveling circus and our dad never taught us much. Never gave us rules until we did something bad and then he yelled and screamed. So my sisters got in trouble, and I've always tried to help them. They say I'm a worthless bum myself, so why would they listen to me? I may ride the rails to my job, but I'm no bum. And look what they do when they get into a tough spot—want me to save them!"

"Are you really a zookeeper?" Larry asked.

"Oh, well, kind of." Buckle seemed to expand, clearly pleased we had asked. "I'm on the weekend park operations crew. Help with the aquarium and the giraffe deck. Some special events, whatever they need me to do."

Buckle explained that he did not have a car. He took the freight train to work from Chicago to Toledo each week. Only once or twice, he said, had it backfired and kept him from making it to work. His eyes were still blinking, and it was hard to not be distracted by them. Maybe he had spent too much time in the bird section of the zoo.

"We actually wanted to talk to you anyway about something else," Larry said. "We wanted to see if you ever met a man by the name of Dr. Bruce Jefferson who was a hobo riding the trains last fall. Or if you know where he went."

Buckle looked down at Larry. "Yeah, I guess I met Bruce a few times. But I don't know much about him. He hung out with another hobo who was in Elkhart a lot. Called Crumb Boss."

"Oh, yes, we talked to Crumb Boss!" I was almost relieved that Buckle didn't know more. It seemed we had more urgent issues to deal with at the moment than talking about the elusive doctor.

"Okay, good." Buckle took his pipe back out of his mouth and I saw him focus on something behind me. "Uh-oh, gentlemen. I think we're caught. There comes a bull."

We all turned to look the way he was facing.

A uniformed security officer was headed our way.

CHAPTER EIGHTEEN

Buckle's Investment

"What's a bull?" Terry asked quietly as our eyes swiveled back to Buckle so we wouldn't be staring at the uniformed man as he approached.

"Railroad police. They have their own police. Probably heard you pounding like crazy."

"Do you think we'll be accused of kidnapping the baby?" Uncle Aaron asked.

Buckle swore and shook his head. "Hope not! Why would they?"

"Well..." Uncle Aaron frowned. "Babies don't normally get on boxcars by themselves."

"Neither did this one," Buckle slurred around his pipe. "We all know Dean put her on."

"Excuse me!" a voice bellowed behind us. "This is railroad

property. Can you tell me what—"

We all turned and looked into the railroad policeman's face, which was drenched with sweat. He had been talking until his eyes fell on the baby and that is the point where he let the sentence lie, as if it was a piece of clothing that didn't quite fit anymore. Apparently, he wasn't expecting to find a baby in a circle of five men and boys beside an empty boxcar.

"Is that a baby?" He finally said, his voice not quite so boisterous as before.

"'Fraid so," Buckle sighed. "We'll be on our way."

"Wait, wait." The uniformed man shook his head back and forth several times as if to recreate the scene. "How do I know you all ain't stealing someone's baby? Does anyone have rights to that child?"

"I do," Buckle said. "She's my niece."

The baby opened her mouth in a mighty yawn, and the pacifier fell down into the rocks. Then she wiggled her mouth around as if she was smiling warmly at the railroad man.

"Do you have any papers to prove it?" The policeman pulled a radio off his belt and held it to his mouth. "Send Tom over between tracks 12 and 13. I need some help."

"Don't got no papers," Buckle said. "Who carries papers with them proving their family connection to their nieces and nephews?"

I knew it was a bad question, and the railroad police officer let him have it.

"Who ignores a no trespassing sign and takes a baby into a

danger zone between two trains? I need you to show me some proof of who owns this baby!" His radio crackled, but he quieted it.

Buckle looked the baby over and shook his head. "Looks like the baby's going to get taken away anyway after all this work around. At least I wouldn't have to surprise my wife. But she is a pretty little thing."

By this time Larry had retrieved the pacifier and brushed it off and put it back in the baby's mouth.

"Sir," Larry said in his confident voice, addressing the officer, "Do you know the rules about changing a baby's diaper? Someone locked us into the boxcar with this baby, so we were trying to take good care of it. But we don't really know how."

The policeman stared at Larry as if he didn't know the rules about anything anymore. He opened his mouth and closed it a few times. Finally, he said, "No. I do not know the rules for changing diapers. But I would like to know what you were doing in this boxcar with a baby. If you hadn't been there, no one could have locked you in."

"We didn't know the baby was in there!" Larry said. "You know, it's dark in boxcars when you step in out of the bright sunshine."

"Yes, I know about boxcars," the officer snapped. "But I've never seen one with a baby in it."

I was afraid Larry would say something smart like, *Well, you should have been in Elkhart this afternoon and you could have!* Thankfully, he didn't.

"I can explain everything," Buckle sighed. "My nephew put the baby in the boxcar to send her to me. It was a family emergency."

"Which one of these boys is your nephew?"

"None. He's back in Elkhart."

At this point, another officer stepped into view from between two cars. As they talked to each other quietly for a bit, Uncle Aaron said, "Where's that note? Find that note."

I had forgotten about the note.

"What note?" Buckle asked.

"Right!" Larry dived into the contents of the pack and seconds later straightened up with the piece of paper. "It's a note for you."

Buckle held the paper out past his rounded stomach and squinted at it, then read it aloud.

"Buckle, you are family. Do something for this child. Our sister is headed for the jug, and I can't take care of her with my own man in there. Take to a mission or church if you have to. Maybe better out of IN. Thanks, Liz."

"That might be enough proof that she belongs to you," Uncle Aaron said. "Look here, sir!"

The officers had turned toward us again, so Uncle Aaron invited them to check out the paper.

They shook their heads in disbelief, and the second one spoke. "This Liz sent this baby out to you in an empty boxcar? That's got to be a crime all its own. Abandonment."

"But they sent these guys along to watch her," Buckle said, pointing to the four of us.

“Still illegal,” the second one mumbled.

“Is that really what happened?” the first one asked.

“We think that is what happened,” Uncle Aaron said. “Although we weren’t given a choice.”

“Look, we don’t have time for this,” the first officer said again. “You’ve got the paper, so take the baby and get out of here. This is railroad property, not a nursery. If you can’t take care of the baby yourself, take it to a mission like the note says. And don’t ever bring a baby onto the trains again.”

“We didn’t—” Larry began, but Uncle Aaron held up a firm hand in front of Larry’s face. Larry stopped talking.

“We’re leaving,” Buckle said. “This way. Help me carry this stuff out of the yard.”

By the time we got to the edge of the yard, we were all panting and sweating. Buckle was beet red again and blinking furiously. I barely noticed the brick buildings rising four and five stories high or the graffiti wrapping around them or the dank odor of trash in the heat.

“We’ve got to get water,” Terry said. “We haven’t had any for a long time.”

“Little service station just other side of this lot,” Buckle gasped. “They’ll have drinks.”

I felt my pocket as if I expected to find money there. Of course, there was none. But I assumed Uncle Aaron had something to buy us drinks.

I did feel the handkerchief and the smooth wooden box from Crumb Boss. For some reason, I pulled it out.

"Recognize this?" I asked Buckle, holding out the package wrapped in cloth.

"Belonged to Bruce, didn't it?" he said.

"To Bruce?" I felt a tingle of suspense in my spine. "You mean the box? The handkerchief was Crumb Boss's."

"Nope, it was Bruce's." Buckle sounded certain. "What do you care about this Bruce guy?"

"We're trying to find him," I said. "He's a surgeon who amputated my leg a few years ago, and I wanted to meet up with him. But we found that he disappeared. Then we heard he came to Elkhart on the train."

"Lost your leg, huh?" Buckle said, staring at my feet like everyone did when they heard this. "Accident?"

"Cancer."

"Oh. Nasty stuff. You going to go find him now after this?"

"We still don't know where he is." I sighed and shook my head. It was pretty pathetic. After all we had been through, we still didn't know. "But we're going to have an appointment with one of the other doctors later this week."

"Why not just go find him?" Buckle asked. He took the handkerchief from me and shook it out. "Isn't his address on here?"

Even Terry stopped his restless fidgeting when Buckle said that. We all stared at him, even as we made our way across the parking lot to the service station. Surely he was out of his mind.

"I thought Crumb Boss wrote that stuff on there," I said. "You think Bruce is in Lansing?"

"Sure. I was there when he handed this kerchief to Crumb

Boss with his address. So he could get him his stuff if he found it."

"Really?" I stared at the writing. "Crumb Boss told us to take this box and handkerchief in case we find him. Because the valuable part was stolen so there was no point to send anything. Why do you think this is his address? We can't even make sense of it."

Buckle pointed to the black markings on the cloth. "Got to think like a hobo then. This here means, *the doctor lives here.*" He pointed to the cross symbol we had seen before. "This here says PO Box and there's those numbers. And like you said, Lansing."

"What?" I saw Larry's head bend over the cloth too. I could sense Uncle Aaron and Terry moving in as well. But they seemed to be in slow motion. "Are you sure?"

"Sure!"

"So I could write him a letter!"

"But Crumb Boss said he was going west," Larry said. "Lansing isn't west."

"Don't know about that," Buckle said. "But that symbol is hobo code for *the doctor lives here.* Hobos don't use that much anymore because there's hospitals and stuff. But I know it because I've studied a couple of those code books."

"Too bad we don't have his locket thing to send back," Terry said.

In the shade of the service station wall, we stopped to reconfigure. I was dumbfounded by the idea that Dr. Jefferson's address might be right there on the handkerchief. I stuffed the handkerchief back into my pocket along with the wooden box. Uncle Aaron gave money to Terry and Larry and told them to go in and buy drinks. Then he and I settled the baby into the box among the blankets.

"Look." Uncle Aaron straightened up from the box. "If you get into a bind with the baby, you could call my sister. Not sure if she could help or not. But it's an idea."

It took me a second to realize that he was talking about my mom. I wanted to say, "Wait, what? You think my mom can take in a baby?" But I said nothing.

"Really? Might not be a bad idea. Here, write me a phone number on this paper." Buckle handed Uncle Aaron the note from Liz, and Uncle Aaron wrote down our home number.

"I don't know if she can take a baby in," Uncle Aaron said. "But she lives close to your sisters and might have an idea of how to help."

"Sure, sure, means a lot," Buckle said. "Thanks for taking care of her in the train too. I want to take care of her. I don't want my niece to have a childhood like we did."

Terry and Larry returned, both guzzling at bottles of drink. They handed drinks to Uncle Aaron and me and Buckle and we all took huge swallows.

"Buckle, can you juggle?" Larry asked. "Since you were with the circus?"

"Oh, sure." Buckle was still breathing hard from our walk. He took another big swallow, then set the bottle down. "Give me your bottle caps."

We handed them over, all four of us.

"That's too many," Larry said.

"It is?" Buckle asked. He tossed one into the air, then another, then another. All four of the caps were sailing through the air with perfect timing and rhythm.

"Wow!" Uncle Aaron said. "I need lessons from you sometime!"

"I used to do this while riding a unicycle." Buckle snapped his hand and suddenly he had collected all the caps. He stooped and picked up a faded bottle cap off the pavement. "My sisters can juggle too." He began again, this time juggling five.

"Wow! I always wanted to juggle four, but I never got there. Five is totally out of my league." Uncle Aaron looked at his watch. "I suppose this isn't the time and place for me to learn. The boys and I need to find a pay phone and figure out how to get back to Elkhart."

"We could hop a train back!" Larry said, as if it was the best idea in the world.

"And we're not going to hop a train," Uncle Aaron said.

"Okay, I just have a couple blocks to walk," Buckle said. "But—"

He coughed and sank a hand into the pocket of his jeans. "Since ya'll been good to me and my family, I'm going to give this to you."

He pulled his hand out of the pocket and opened his fingers. Sunlight flashed on something silver.

CHAPTER NINETEEN

Mom Gets the Update

"What's that?" Larry asked.

"Goes in that wooden box," he said, pointing to my pocket.

"What?" I pulled the box out. "That's Dr. Jefferson's? Where'd you find it?"

Buckle shifted a little.

"I just lifted it outta there last night when I came through the Elkhart Hobo Jungle and no one was lookin'. I didn't even know about this baby at the time, but my sisters have been short on funds, and couldn't see as how Bruce would need it. Thought I'd sell it somewhere cause they was saying it was an expensive piece. But—" he waved his hand "—ain't mine. And you all can get it back to him once you find him."

I stared at Buckle in disbelief and watched the links of the fine silver chain pour out of his hand into mine. "Thanks," I gulped. "We'll get it back to him for sure."

"Yeah, wow," Uncle Aaron said. "You helped us a lot. Showed us the address and now this. By the way, is there any way we could...help your sisters? Especially Dean's mom?"

Buckle sighed again. "I don't know myself." He was still blinking but I was almost used to it.

The baby whimpered in the box. Terry fumbled in his pocket. He dangled his length of thin rope over the baby, and she clamped a tiny fist onto it.

"I knew there would be a need for my rope!" Terry looked as smug as if he had just solved the problem of world hunger.

Buckle turned from watching the baby with the rope toy to Uncle Aaron. "My sister—Dean's mom—always liked throwing parties. Not even drinking parties, but nice Christian parties for children with games and candy and pizza. She did that for the circus urchins whenever she got a big tip, and our dad always told her she was wasting her money. But she really liked to make people happy. When her husband worked for the clock company, they had neighborhood block parties. And I think she hates it now that she's poor and can't invite people much. But, there's not much you can do about that. It's the one thing she was good at."

Buckle picked up the box with the baby.

"One more question!" Larry, of course. "Why didn't Crumb Boss tell us Dr. Jefferson's address was on there? That seems weird."

Buckle shrugged. "He's a hobo. Why would a hobo work

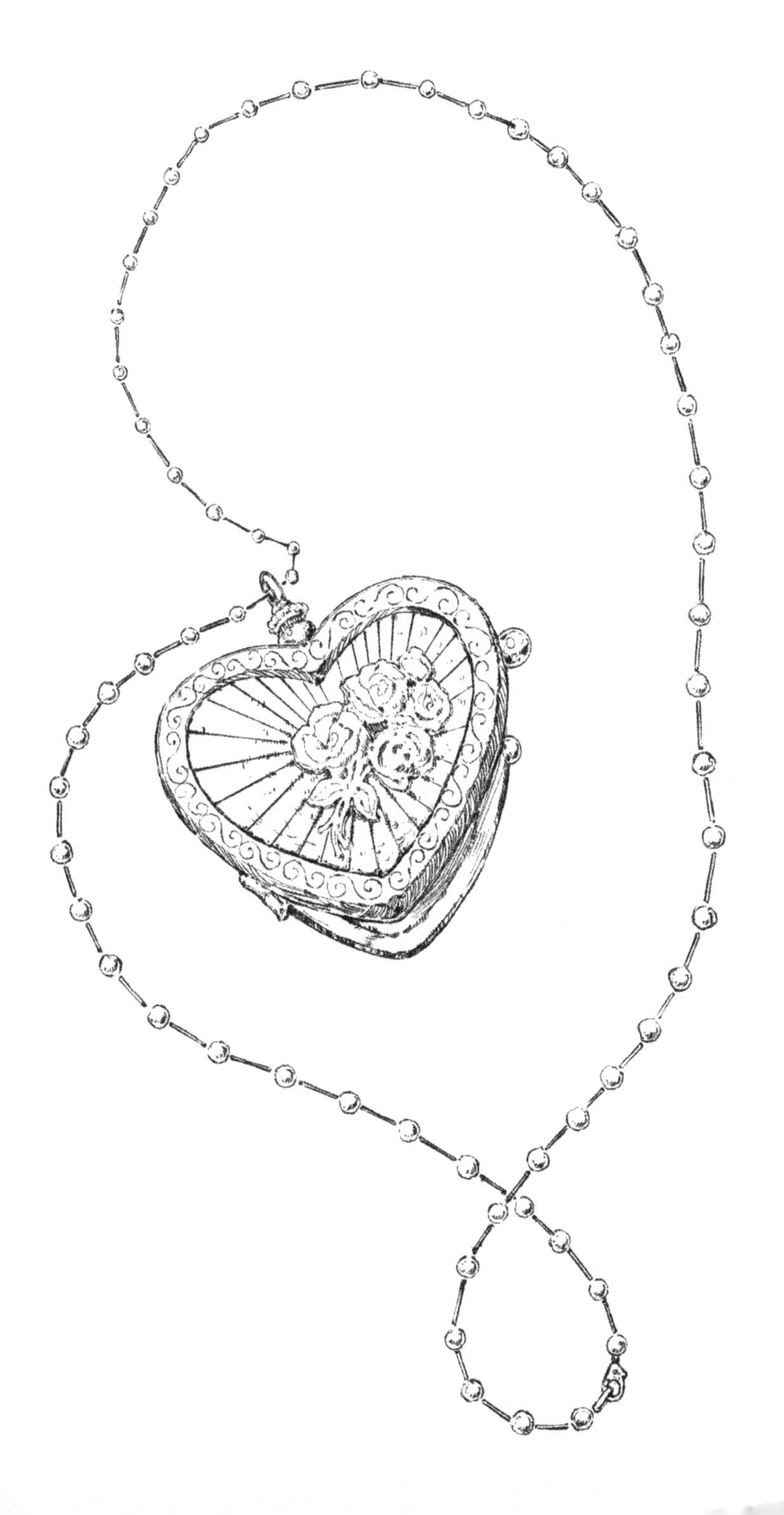

harder than he has to? You didn't ask, why should he tell? So long!" And with that he disappeared around the corner of the service station. It was like he was afraid if he stayed too long, he would ask for the locket back. Terry's rope went with him, but Terry shrugged as if it was a small price to pay for such a weighty breakthrough.

I opened my hand and looked at it. It was a heart-shaped locket that opened on a soft, noiseless hinge. It was lined with velvet and there was a small curl of hair inside. My brothers and Uncle Aaron peered at it too.

"Better not lose the hair," Uncle Aaron said. "It's probably a sweet memory to someone."

"It could be from a pet rabbit," Terry suggested.

"What do you know about romance?" Larry asked.

"Not much." Uncle Aaron laughed. "Just a hunch. Put it in that box, Gary, and wrap it back up and don't lose it. I see a phone booth across the street. Let's step over."

"Can we get more drinks while you do that?" Terry asked. "We'll pay you back."

"Sure."

While Larry and Terry went back in for drinks, I followed Uncle Aaron. I would not miss this conversation. Mom was probably really wondering where we were or at least why we hadn't called.

"What time is it?" I asked.

Uncle Aaron glanced at his watch. "Almost 2:30. Think your

mom is frantic?"

"Probably."

Uncle Aaron grabbed the receiver from the phone booth and dropped a quarter into the metal slot. I heard it rattle into the inner bank of the phone.

"Punch the numbers for me, will you? Don't forget 1-219."

With my index finger, I pressed the square number buttons, starting with 1 and the area code as Uncle Aaron reminded me. Uncle Aaron held the receiver between us so we could both hear the phone ringing. His other hand rested on the silver cord that connected the receiver to the box. We leaned against opposite sides of the phone booth as if we were exhausted from all the sitting we had done that morning.

"Hello?" It was Mom's voice.

"Hi, Mom!"

"Gary? Where are you? I've been so worried about you!" Her voice choked up. "I just called Dad again and to make a plan to go looking for you."

Uncle Aaron laughed. "It would be a while before you found us."

"We're in Chicago!" I couldn't help breaking into a grin at the thought of Mom's face. I wished I could see it.

"You're WHAT?" Mom asked. "Aaron. Surely you could have called me before taking them all the way out there! You didn't join the circus after all, did you?"

"No ma'am," Uncle Aaron said. "Well, I guess it depends on what you call the circus. And, I confess in this case I could not call you. We were locked in a boxcar that took off out of the Elkhart yard."

"What?" A stranger might have thought that *What?* was Mom's favorite word, the way this was going. "Aaron, are you serious? Is everyone okay? Where are Terry and Larry? I haven't heard them."

"They're in the service station getting drinks," I said. "It's really hot. We were afraid we were going to die of thirst before someone found us, but thankfully, we got out."

"Oh, Gary, I'm so glad to hear your voice. I need to call Dad and let him know you are all right. But wait, how are you getting back?"

"Don't worry," Uncle Aaron said. "I already have a plan. We'll get to a South Shore station and be back in South Bend before you know it. Do you think you could come pick us up?"

"Well, sure," Mom said. "Call me before you get on, so I know when to expect you. Are you really serious? You got locked in a boxcar?"

"Yes, by Dean," I said. "And we haven't even told you about the baby."

Uncle Aaron and I grinned wildly at each other across the phone. *This* was the fun part of our escapade.

"The what?" Mom said.

A recorded voice announced that the call was about to be cut off unless we deposited more money.

"Got to go, I'm running out of money!" Uncle Aaron said. "We'll call you before we head for South Bend! We need to find some food first too."

"Okay, be careful! I'm anxious to see you and hear the rest of the story."

The call cut off. I could imagine Mom slamming the receiver down on our rotary telephone and then grabbing it up again all in the same motion to call Dad. *I think they said something about a baby, but maybe I heard wrong.*

We asked the gas station attendant for directions and took a taxi to the nearest South Shore station. To our surprise, it was the same one we had come to when we visited the Oriental Institute. Uncle Aaron bought us all tickets, but we saw it was still a half hour until the train arrived. So we hustled over to Dairy Queen and got something to eat. The whole day was turning out to be pretty expensive. Uncle Aaron made a quick call to Mom to tell her when our train was expected in South Bend so she could come pick us up. He was hanging up the phone when the train blew in. We clattered on, food and all.

"You know," Uncle Aaron said once we were settled on the train and dipping ravenously into our bags of food, "maybe we should have told your mom more about the baby. What if Buckle calls her for help before we even get home?"

"Surely not," Larry said. "He cares about the baby a little at least, if he agreed to take him in the first place."

"Her," I said.

"Oh, right."

"Just because you care about a baby doesn't mean you know how to take care of it, does it?" Uncle Aaron grinned at us and then yawned. "I might need to take a nap."

"Aren't you glad you didn't join the circus, Uncle Aaron?" Larry asked. "It doesn't sound like it was a good place for Buckle to grow up."

"Yeah, that's what my parents told me when I was determined to join it. They were right." He nodded sleepily. "Terry, I'm wondering how you're feeling about Dean. Still needing to practice long-suffering?"

"Huh." Terry sighed and spooned up the last of his ice cream. "Yeah, so I get it that he might have been looking out for the baby. But it was still a mean trick to play on us."

"He knew that Buckle would be waiting for us in Chicago." Larry snapped up a stray french fry.

"He *thought* he would be." Terry pointed a finger in the air as if he were pointing to a blackboard. "He didn't *know*. What if something would have happened and he didn't make it? We would have died of heat and thirst."

"I think Buckle would have alerted the authorities to look for the baby." Uncle Aaron sipped Coke through a straw.

"Well, sure. But what about this." Terry wasn't finished. "Why wouldn't Dean just ask us if we would ride to Chicago to keep an eye on the baby? We could have done that with the door open."

"Would we have agreed?" Uncle Aaron asked. "I doubt it."

"Maybe he didn't think about it much." I crumpled my cheeseburger wrapper into a small ball and threw it into one of our paper bags. "That was the best cheeseburger I have ever had in my life."

"Yeah, maybe Dean doesn't make an outline of points for every decision he makes, like Gary here." Uncle Aaron crumpled his wrapper and threw it at me, hitting me squarely in the forehead. "I agree about the cheeseburgers. And no butterflies this time! By the way, Larry, I am fed up!"

Larry rolled his eyes.

"Don't roll your eyes, Larry. That encourages him to say it more!" I held on to the crumpled ball and decided to bide my time with it for a bit. "One thing I don't understand. How did Dean get that moniker drawn on the car soon enough that Old Fish could see it and come let us know? Did he have the baby there the whole time?"

"It wasn't that long," Terry said. "Old Fish probably marched right over."

"Maybe half an hour though until we got there. Maybe the baby was sleeping." I fired the paper wad at Uncle Aaron.

Uncle Aaron twisted to the side, then jerked in pain as his back caught, which made me feel bad. It seemed to make him serious too, from what he said next.

"This whole experience is a great example of why we need God to help us with things like long-suffering." Uncle Aaron carefully eased back to his previous position, picked up the wrapper ball, and threw it in the trash bag. "It gets really frustrating when someone hurts you or tricks you over and over again. I don't think there's a good way to deal with things like that other than by asking God for help."

"Yeah, that's how I felt when Old Fish was talking and talking without saying anything yesterday," I said. "By the way, Uncle Aaron. Can you find a person by having their post office box? Do you think we could track down Dr. Jefferson if we got to Lansing?"

Uncle Aaron opened his mouth, then rubbed his shoulder and closed his mouth. It was like he was pretty sure of the answer but not sure how I would take it. Finally, he opened it again. "I think it's kind of impossible to track someone down by having their post office box number, unless you sit in the post office all day waiting and watching. Or unless one of the post office workers has some mercy on you."

"It still helps to know it though," Larry said. "You can write to him!"

I nodded. "I guess that's probably the best thing to do. But I'd really like to go there and try to find him."

"Sure, let's do it." Uncle Aaron threw his empty Coke cup in the paper bag. "It can't hurt, as long as you don't get your hopes up too high. Your dad said Lansing is only about an hour away."

Mom was parked at the curb when we pulled into the South Bend train station. She listened in stunned amazement to our tale as she drove us home. For a second, as Larry explained our predicament with the baby, her hands fell limply around the steering wheel.

"I should have let you drive, Aaron," she said. "I don't know if I can handle this. None of you know *anything* about babies."

"Oh, we did a great job!" Terry said.

"Terry, you didn't do anything with the baby at all!" Larry

said.

"Yes I did! I let her have my rope. That was a huge sacrifice!"

"Okay." Mom's voice really was a little shaky, and I was hoping she wouldn't crash the car. "Can you skip ahead in the story and tell me if the baby is okay?"

We reassured her that as far as we knew, the baby was fine.

Mom took us into Elkhart so we could get Uncle Aaron's car. As we pulled up to the road that led to the rail yard, I heard Uncle Aaron say, "Oh, no. Maybe our drama isn't over for the day."

In the back seat, the three of us knocked our heads together trying to look out the windshield. Uncle Aaron's car was surrounded by police vehicles with flashing lights.

CHAPTER TWENTY

The Missing Details

"Pull off here and we'll get out," Uncle Aaron said. "Or maybe just me."

"Oh, we have to get out too!" Terry said. "Maybe this is about the baby, and we are witnesses just as much as you!"

We all spilled out of the back of the car. Mom frowned and said she was going to wait to see what happened because she certainly was not going to lose track of us again.

The four of us approached Uncle Aaron's car slowly. He had parked it as close to the trees as he could to pick up some shade in the stifling heat and to stay off the road. I noticed that the uniformed men surrounding the car were both Elkhart city police and railroad police. I saw the enormous guard we had met at the top of the stairs in the train yard the day before. Instead of a pencil, he was carrying a flashlight just his size. I had never seen one so huge. He saw us coming and came our way, his eyes on Uncle Aaron.

"This your Camaro?"

"Yes, sir, it is."

"Okay. Can you open the trunk for us please?"

"Sure." Uncle Aaron's hand sank into his pants pocket, and I heard the jangle of keys. "Can I ask why?"

"Just checking the area." The man's huge head turned toward the trunk of the car. "Elkhart police arrested a woman yesterday for drug trafficking, and her baby appears to be missing. Seems to be a connection with the rail yard here. Trunks are always a concern, especially in abandoned cars. Especially on hot days. But I guess this car isn't abandoned anymore."

"No, we were gone for a bit." Uncle Aaron glanced back at us. "Stay back so you aren't in the way."

He walked over to the trunk and opened it. The policemen shone their flashlights around the corners, nodded, and allowed him to close it.

"Okay, no problem." The huge guard nodded to Uncle Aaron. "No further questions."

Uncle Aaron cleared his throat. "Um, we might…that is, I'm not sure what information you were given, but we might be able to help you out. It would mean admitting that we trespassed on railroad property, I'm afraid. But we did find a baby in a boxcar."

Of course, when the guard heard this, he told us to come with them up to the rail yard for a chat. We explained this to Mom, who sighed and nodded.

"Will they be able to come home for supper?" Mom asked the big man.

"As far as we know, ma'am." He moved the large flashlight from one huge hand to the other.

Aaron drove his own car, but we were escorted front and back by official vehicles. We pulled up beside the same block building as before and went back up the outside stairs and into the security office of the rail yard. The large security officer ducked to get in the door. The room was a tight fit with several wooden desks, the map cabinet I had seen earlier with corners of maps sticking out, and all of us, plus the officers. The big guard sat in his corner of the room as if he were wearing it. He flipped the switch on the large metal fan behind him, turning it on before he sat in his desk chair.

Uncle Aaron told the story, with the rest of us adding details. The officers scribbled on notepads.

When Uncle Aaron wrapped up the story with the baby going home with Buckle, several of the officers shook their heads.

"You know," one said, "you could press charges against this Dean boy for locking you in. But that's going to mean that you admit you were trespassing."

"We don't want to get Dean into trouble anyway." Uncle Aaron shifted and rubbed his back, wincing. "He didn't abandon the baby. He protected her by locking us in with her. The baby is his cousin."

"Interesting." The railroad security officer we had met the day before chewed on his large pencil and looked at the city police. "I don't know what you all want to do with this, but I don't think I need to send any of these people to jail. They were trespassing, but it sounds like that was a good thing in this case." He took the pencil out of his mouth and bit his lip, as if he felt compelled to chew on something at all times. "But I don't recommend you do any more of it," he said quickly with a glance at us.

"Oh, we won't," Larry said. "We found our hobo anyway."

"How did you find out a baby was missing?" Uncle Aaron asked. "Or am I not allowed to ask?"

"We arrested the mother for criminal drug activity," one said. "And she said she gave the baby to her nephew to dispose of and that it was none of our business. We got a description of the nephew and found out that a boy about his age was seen in this area with a box this morning and then leaving later without a box."

"I see. Thanks for letting us know," Uncle Aaron said. "Are we okay to leave?"

"Fill out this form," the city police officer said. "Just in case we need to contact you later. But it sounds like the baby is with family, so there's not much we can do about that."

We left the rail yard and parked beside the Hobo Jungle again. We ran over to the cluster of trees to look for Crumb Boss. But there was no one under the blue tarp. The fire was cold. I couldn't even see a plastic fork in the dirt, but I don't know why I looked for it. It was surely in Crumb Boss's pocket at that moment or combing his hair.

"I guess that's how hobos work," Uncle Aaron said. "They come and they go. At least we know we have Dr. Jefferson's address."

"If Buckle is right," Larry said.

"If Buckle is right," Uncle Aaron agreed.

We piled around the supper table that night, exhausted and thankful, and dug into the potato salad and corn on the cob Mom had prepared.

"Guess who I saw this afternoon," Dad said.

The chewing in the room nearly stopped as we looked at him.

"Dean?" I asked.

Dad nodded, sprinkling salt on his corn cob with a practiced flick of the wrist. "He came and confessed everything."

We looked at Dad, amazed.

"He apologized?" Terry's fork clattered to his plate, sending a piece of potato nosediving into the corn cob platter.

Dad went on. "I think he was worried that he would be liable for the crime if anything happened to any of you, and he wanted us to know where you were so that nothing bad would happen. Dean said his aunt brought her baby to his mom's place this weekend. She told them that she was sure she would be arrested soon, and she didn't want the baby going to the authorities as well. She wanted Dean's mom to take the baby, but she refused. After Dean's aunt was arrested at the restaurant, their brother Buckle agreed to take the baby if they bring him out to him. He had just been there at the Elkhart yard, but they weren't able to reach him by phone until he got back to Chicago. And since they were all familiar with hopping on trains, they decided that was the way they could do it."

"Brilliant," Terry mumbled.

"Dean said he biked to the yard and got one of the yard workers to tell him which train was the one going to Chicago."

"Wait, he did bike?" I looked up from my potato salad. "With a baby in a box?"

"No, keep listening," Dad said. "He picked an empty car, drew his uncle's symbol on it, and then biked over to the graveyard to wait for his mom who was going to bring the baby. She brought it, and Dean asked his mom if he shouldn't go along. Dean's mom said she would ground him for weeks if he went with the baby because she needed his help, and that she was going to wait right there at the graveyard for him to return. Dean told me he was afraid that he would go to prison for abandoning the baby in the car. So, when he saw that you were looking for the car too, he decided to see if he could trap you inside. But then he was afraid you would make a bunch of noise in Elkhart and be discovered, and the baby would never get to its destination."

"See! We should have pounded!" Terry looked at Uncle Aaron.

"No, we shouldn't have." Larry rolled his eyes at Terry. "It all worked out, and the baby got to the right place."

"Well, we were miserable."

"Then Dean wasn't really trying to be mean to us," Uncle Aaron was sitting at the end of the table across from Dad. "I wondered."

"He actually thought it out pretty well." I remembered our

conversation on the train home where I had said that maybe Dean didn't think too much at all. "It still wasn't a nice thing to do. But..."

"What could he do?" Larry said, shrugging, which was exactly what I was thinking.

What a terrible predicament to be in!

"He could have taken her to the police," Dad said. "But apparently the family is very determined to keep the baby with a family member. Although why they thought they had to get her to a different state, I don't know."

Mom had been calmly eating a piece of corn, which she now put down on the finished cobs platter. "I have a story too. After I left you at the train yard, I went to the grocery store for mustard for the potato salad. The cashiers there said that the waitress working at Rocky's Riverside Restaurant told police they couldn't take her because she had a baby to care for. The owners of the restaurant were kind of horrified by the whole commotion, of course. They only hired her a few weeks ago because they were desperate for help. But they didn't know she had a drug business on the side. I did hear a rumor that she showered the restaurant with ketchup yesterday."

"Oh, that's what it was!" I brought my hand down on the edge of the table with a smack. "I knew I heard her voice before. Of course, I had. We all had. She was yelling in the apartment with Dean's mom."

"You must be good at recognizing voices," Uncle Aaron said. "I never thought about it."

"And that's why Dean ran away from the restaurant!" I picked up my fork again. "He was going to tell his mom that she got arrested."

"Things are always so much easier to see after you hear the whole story," Uncle Aaron said. "Maybe Dean was watching the restaurant on purpose to see if the police would come there."

We talked about the case, filling Mom and Dad in on some of the details. Larry explained that the lady had covered her heart tattoo with makeup. I suggested that she was wearing extra clothes to look bigger, less like her description. We also told them that Buckle and his two sisters had grown up with a traveling circus and a negligent father. And that Dean's mom, who we now knew was named Liz, and the baby's mom, could juggle like Buckle.

Terry looked at Uncle Aaron. "Don't you feel stupid about giving her extra tip money now?"

Uncle Aaron took a bite of potato salad and ate it slowly before answering with his own question. "Should I?"

This question hung in the air for a while. A fly landed on the finished corn cobs' platter and Larry waved it away. Finally, Uncle Aaron said, "I don't really think I do feel stupid about that. It might be the only nice thing anyone has done for her in a long time."

"Except for Dean," I said. "Dean took care of the baby for her."

"Right." Uncle Aaron nodded. "I guess he did. Thanks for the good meal, Bella. I'm fed up!"

Just then, we all heard a knock on the door.

CHAPTER TWENTY-ONE

Tuesday Night

Dean stood on the porch, his hood around his face.

Larry had gone to the door alone. He was the youngest in the family, so we often made him run the errands.

"Mom!" he yelled. "Dean's here! Can he come eat with us?"

"Sure!" Mom jumped up and hurried to the cupboard. "Slide down, Terry. We can put him on the corner between you and Uncle Aaron."

We slid down so there would be room for Dean, which made the silverware rattle against the plate. But Larry came back to the kitchen alone.

"He doesn't want to come in. Can he have some of those cookies I made yesterday?"

Mom grabbed the cookie box and went back to the door with Larry. Neither of them could convince him to stay, but he agreed to take a handful of cookies.

Uncle Aaron stacked the extra place setting together and slid it onto the counter behind him. Terry and I spread out again, and Larry and Mom sat down across from us.

"He wanted to know if we got home okay." Larry slowly buttered his second ear of corn. "He acted like he was mad when I yelled to Mom about him staying for supper. Why would he be mad about that?"

"I'm guessing he was embarrassed." Uncle Aaron leaned back in his chair and sighed. "He might be a lasting offense for you all for a while."

"Easy symbol for the long-suffering project," I said. "A train car."

"Isn't there a verse that says, 'Beareth all things?' That could be our Bible verse." Larry waved his hand toward the saltshaker which was sitting close to Dad. "I feel like we had to bear a lot with Dean the last two days."

"I feel like I'm needing to bear a lot right now with your table manners." Dad picked up the salt and handed it to Larry. "Do you just wave at the item you want someone to pass?"

"Oops," Larry said. "I was too busy talking about long-suffering, I guess."

Next Dad picked up the Bible on the buffet behind him. "Do you want me to help you out since you had a hard day?"

We all agreed that we would be happy for some assistance.

"Your verse is in 1 Corinthians 13, the love chapter. It says that love 'beareth all things, believeth all things, hopeth all things, endureth all things.'"

"We endured." Uncle Aaron raised an eyebrow. "But maybe not as hopefully as we should have."

Larry wrote the verse out on Mom's chart.

"Do you think anyone will ever see our drawings on the boxcar floor?" I imagined how nice it would be for someone to find our symbols.

"Like someone else who is trapped?" Terry asked.

"No, of course not!" I said. "Some railroad worker or something."

"Who was the most long-suffering person today?" Mom asked. "Of the four of you?"

"Uncle Aaron," the three of us said together.

"Oh no." Sincere shock spread across Uncle Aaron's face. "I got really bent out of shape and started snapping at the boys. Definitely not me. Terry had a few choice words for Dean. And Larry kept reminding us of the horrible deaths of people trapped in boxcars. I'm thinking the award might go to Gary."

"Oh, I wasn't very long-suffering," I said. "Unless it counts that I suffered for a long time."

But I couldn't talk them out of it.

Just as they voted me to be the most long-suffering person for that day, the phone rang.

Uncle Aaron tensed. "What if it's Buckle?"

Dad walked to the phone and picked up the receiver. "Hello?" A pause. "Oh, yes! They mentioned meeting you today."

"It's Buckle!" Terry hissed.

"We met a lot of people today." Uncle Aaron said this slowly, as if he too was pretty sure it was Buckle.

"How old is the baby?" Dad asked.

We froze. He was asking Mom to take the baby.

"Would it be legal for me to take the baby?" Mom whispered to us. She looked kind of interested and kind of scared.

"Oh good! Glad to hear that."

"The baby's all right!" Larry hissed.

Dad was quiet for a moment. "Okay. I'll talk to my wife. Thanks for letting us know." Dad let the receiver clunk back onto the telephone and turned slowly as if to prolong our suspense. "Buckle says his wife is getting along great with the baby. He thought you might want to know. She's doing well."

We stared at him for a while. Then Terry clapped his hands above his head and let loose. "Hurray! We kept a baby alive today! We're heroes!"

Uncle Aaron laughed and shook his head. "I'm thanking God that Buckle didn't miss finding us on the train."

"Wait, how old is the baby?" I raised a hand. "We couldn't decide between one year old and a few days old."

"Three months." Dad glanced at Mom, studying her face. "But, Buckle did say that his wife is having surgery on both hands in a few weeks. She doesn't know if she can take care of the baby during that time."

"Hmmm," Mom said, and that was all she would say.

"Thanks again for the meal, Bella. If it's okay, I have an errand to run." Uncle Aaron rose to his feet. "Anyone want to join me? Someone gave me a Pizza Hut gift certificate for my last birthday, and I never used it. I want to take it to its new home."

Somehow, all three of us boys summoned the energy to go with him. Ten minutes later, we were standing outside the door with the number 8, and Uncle Aaron was knocking. Dean came to the door himself, with a cookie in his hand and what looked like an entire one in his mouth too.

"I brought something for your mom," Uncle Aaron said.

"She's not home." A piece of cookie fell out of his mouth and dropped onto the threshold.

"Okay, no problem. You can give it to her. Buckle said she likes hosting parties." He handed over the gift certificate. "Someone gave it to me a long time ago, and I haven't gotten around to using it. I would like to see it go to a good home."

"Buckle said she was really good at hosting parties," I added.

"Yes, she is." Dean's eyes lit up with happiness. "I love her parties!"

"Okay, we'll be off," Uncle Aaron said. "I hope you have a fun party."

"Stop by whenever!" Larry said.

Dean lifted the cookie in one hand and pointed to it with the other. "I might do that."

We were all laughing as we headed down the stairs. The evening sun had pushed through the smudged glass of the front door, bathing the main hallway in yellow light that was almost hopeful.

"No offense," Terry said when we were outside. "But we would have made a good new home for your pizza gift certificate too."

"Maybe." Uncle Aaron picked three small stones off the parking lot and began juggling them as he walked to the car. "But I like its new home better."

That night we sat in our living room and discussed the whole story again. Dad, in the recliner, Mom in the rocking chair, and Uncle Aaron on the couch. Terry and I were sprawled on the floor, and Larry was in the library with the hobo codes book, but still close enough to be in the conversation.

"So, what's the next step?" Dad tossed the newspaper to Uncle Aaron who was waiting for it.

"Cookies?" Terry, rearranging on the carpet, smiled at his own joke.

"About the manhunt." Dad gave Terry a nudge with his foot. "Are you going to send Dr. Jefferson a letter to that address?"

"I just want to go find him!" I said. "You know we saw this 1A after Lansing. Maybe that's an apartment number that can point us in the right direction."

Dad frowned. "Lansing is a big place. There are probably fifty or a hundred apartment buildings with a 1A. Or it could be half of a house."

"Wait, let me see that," Mom said. "It seems strange to me that the apartment number would come after the city name."

I handed her the handkerchief.

"Yeah," Larry agreed. "That's where the state goes."

"There's no 1A state though," I said.

"It's not a *one*," Mom said. "It's the letter *I*. Look, there's a *1* in the address and that's shaped differently."

We all leaped off the floor to look at it. "Sure enough!" Larry said. "But Lansing is in Michigan, so what does IA mean?"

"Iowa!" I shouted. "That would explain why Crumb Boss said Bruce is going west. But is there a town named Lansing in Iowa, too?"

"He didn't write a zip code on there, did he?" Dad walked to the library and reached up to a top shelf of the bookcase. He came back with an atlas and a smaller book that said *Zip Code Directory*. He sat back in his recliner and opened the atlas to the index.

"How was Crumb Boss going to mail it without a zip code?" Larry asked.

"Probably ask at the post office." Dad flipped the pages. "Lansing, Iowa. Sure enough. I thought there was but couldn't remember for sure. Look, right here by the Mississippi River. Small town. Let me find the zip code in case you want to send him something by mail."

"That totally solves it!" I leaped up and grabbed the atlas while dad opened the zip code directory. "Let's go to Iowa!"

"We still don't know where he lives." Uncle Aaron shifted the newspaper so he could see us. "Remember what I said. You can't find someone just because you know their post office box."

Uncle Aaron's realism couldn't dampen my zeal. I stared with fascination at the word *Lansing*, about an inch below the top of

the state where the land turned into Minnesota. The town sat on the western edge of the fat blue ribbon of Mississippi River dividing Iowa from Wisconsin.

"When people don't want to be found, they only give you their post office box." Dad's finger moved down the column in the zip code directory. "I think it's a strategy used by people who are running from the law. "But in such a small town...maybe. Here's the zip code. 52151."

Terry jumped up and went to the library for his rope-drawing notebook and wrote down the zip code. His helpfulness shocked me, and I decided he must be as excited as me.

"When did you say he left here?" Dad closed the directory. "Last fall? Maybe he's still there. Maybe not. At any rate, there's no way I can take a road trip right now with the shop so busy. I don't even think I can make it to Chicago for your appointment."

"Well," Mom said. "I have an idea. Uncle Aaron goes with us to the appointment. If the doctor tells us where Dr. Jefferson is, the search is over. If he doesn't, and you still want to go to Iowa, I'll take the train home and Uncle Aaron can take you. What do you think, Ferguson? Am I out of my mind?"

Dad shrugged. "It's fine with me. I wish I could go. But I guess the next best thing is to send you with Aaron."

A dead silence of complete shock descended on the room.

"Wait." Uncle Aaron sat up on the couch with a puzzled expression, the newspaper fluttering in front of him. "Are you trying to tell me you still trust me to be the chaperone after today?"

We all burst out laughing.

"No, I'm serious!"

"It was a strange day you had," Mom said. "But it wasn't really your fault. And when I said you could go to Iowa, I meant by car. Not by freight train."

"Oh, I see!" Uncle Aaron winked at us. "I thought you wanted us to practice our hobo skills."

"I thought you wanted us to go with a traveling circus," I said.

"You *are* a traveling circus," Mom said. "But remember. You won't need to go to Iowa if we get good information at the doctor's office."

"This is the first time I'm not sure if I want good information." I folded the handkerchief carefully, wrapping it around the wooden box which now held Dr. Jefferson's silver locket. "A trip to the Mississippi River sounds fun."

"Whatever you do," Dad said. "Don't fall in or drown or get locked in somewhere or find any international fugitive. Or get terrified of farm pigs."

"Aw, come on," Terry said. "We're always reliable."

"You're always reliable to make me feel good about my checkers game." Uncle Aaron threw down the newspaper. "Want to play?"

Find the rest of the books in this series as they come out by visiting *www.katrinahooverlee.com* and subscribing to our email list.

About the Author

Hi! I'm Katrina.

When I was a little younger than Terry, Gary, and Larry, I created them to help pass the time doing chores. I told stories about the boys to my brother Scott as we weeded the driveway, worked in the produce patch, or folded laundry. Occasionally, Mom even banned the storytelling because it took us longer to do our work if I was telling stories!

For about a decade, I wrote books for adults, including *Blue Christmas, Shatterproof, Captain Garrison,* and *From the White*

House to the Amish. You can browse my books at my online store, as well as in many other stores.

Now my husband Marnell and I have a child of our own. Upon the suggestion of my aunt Virginia, I am returning to my own childhood and bringing Terry, Gary, and Larry back to life. My husband lost his leg to cancer as a young boy, so the stories reflect his childhood as well.

My husband and I currently live in Elkhart, Indiana, close to the fictional town of Stratford. I named the boys' town after my hometown in Wisconsin. It is set on the St. Joseph River, right between South Bend and Elkhart. Although it is real in this story, do not come to northern Indiana looking for the town of Stratford. You will not find it!

To keep up to date on more books in this series, subscribe to my email list at *www.katrinahooverlee.com.* You may also write to Katrina Lee, The Brady Street Boys, PO Box 2155, Elkhart, IN 46515 or email me *Katrina@500-words.com.*

Did you enjoy *Tricked on the Tracks*?
Are you able to leave an online review?

Today, many people buy books online. Your review is crucial to help others know what this book is like. No matter where you got your book, if you could take a few moments to give an honest review on Amazon, Barnes and Noble, or another online store, you will help us a lot!

Thanks!

Marnell and Katrina Lee

Many Thanks!

- My husband Marnell, always full of tricky ideas to make each book better.
- My daughter Anina, who went with me to the Elkhart train yard for research.
- Editors and Proofreaders: Gina Martin, Gideon Yutzy, Sara Nolt, Krista Mullet, Sherilyn Yoder. Thanks for saving this book.
- Kenneth Stone, former railroad employee at the Elkhart Yard. Thank you for sharing your stories and answering my questions. Of note, while Kenneth confirmed the existence of the Hobo Jungle by the underpass, he did tell me it was no longer in use in the 1980s. For the sake of this fictional account, I brought the hobos into the story anyway. However, I want to be clear that this was creative license. Hobos traveled the rails much more in the decades prior to the 1980s.
- The many beta readers from around the country and the world who helped make the book better. See the following list of names.

Beta Readers

Andrea Peachey
Chad Weaver
Vance A Kolb
Tivon Kolb
Charlie Bergen
Dimitri Bergen
Leah Bergen
Jotham Wagler
Bonica Teresa Reimer
Sami Duerksen
Brant
Valerie
Tara
Adriel
Tyrell Rosenberry
Robin Loewen
Elisabeth Loewen
Kaylene Penner
Vinton Martin
Katelyn Zimmerman
Daryn Kauffman
Chad Kauffman
Kaitlyn Siegrist
Marian Martin
Adrielle Frost
Elliot Mast
Autumn Derstine
Molly Derstine
Rebekah Fehr
Erika Leinbach
Julie Leinbach
Genevie Leinbach
Jeffrey Byler
Jeremy Witmer
Brooke Mummau
Sophia Petre
Jana Gerber
Cole Miller
Krissy Petre
Cody Graber
Charissa Martin
Deborah Brubaker
Wade Brubaker
Miguel Stoltzfus
Ellana Erb
Curtis Abe Friesen
Durrell Miller
Jennalyn Hursh

Adam Loewen
Alyssa Hoover
Rachel Yoder
Shayla Horst
Ashton Horst
Weston Zamy
Ashlyn Horst
Emily Kauffman
Kurtis Loewen
Christopher and Zachary Sensenig
Haylee Yoder
Georgiana Graber
Sylvia Dyck
Monica Yoder
Darren
Jeneva Yoder
Arwen Zook
Ginevera Zook
Tristan Zook
Kiana Good
Ashlyn Zimmerman
LeAnne Martin
Yalonda Miller
Zach Gingerich
Victoria Miller
Jensen Yoder
Colson Yoder